796.323

13072

	DATE DUE		

THIS GAME'S THE BEST!

THIS GAME'S THE BEST!

GEORGE KARL

THIS GAME'S THE BEST!

SO WHY DON'T THEY QUIT SCREWING WITH IT?

AND DON YAEGER

THIS GAME'S THE BEST!

ST. MARTIN'S PRESS ≋ NEW YORK

Design by Songhee Kim

Library of Congress Cataloging-in-Publication Data

Karl, George Matthew.
    This game's the best! (so why don't they quit screwing with it?) / George Karl with Don Yaeger.
      p. cm.
    ISBN 0-312-15671-5
    1. Basketball—United States. 2. National Basketball Association.
  I. Yaeger, Don. II. Title.
  GV885.7.K37 1997
  796.323'0973—dc21   97-2354
                                         CIP

First Edition: May 1997

10 9 8 7 6 5 4 3 2 1

TO DAD: YOUR LOVE AND CONFIDENCE ARE WHY I'M HERE.

THANKS FOR ALWAYS BEING THERE.

GK

TO JIM: TRUE FRIEND, UNFAILING SUPPORTER, AND

SECOND FATHER. I HOPE I'VE MADE YOU PROUD.

DY

CONTENTS

ONE	REDEMPTION	1
TWO	A BOY FROM PITTSBURGH	29
THREE	PLAYING FOR COACH	45
FOUR	THOSE ABA DAYS	67
FIVE	TOWNS YOU'VE NEVER HEARD OF	81
SIX	TOO YOUNG TO KNOW BETTER	101
SEVEN	MY OWN PURGATORY	123
EIGHT	THE RESCUE	147
NINE	LOSING AND LEARNING	159
TEN	SHAWN AND GARY	181
ELEVEN	COACHING IN THE '90S	197
TWELVE	A FIX FOR THE GAME	229
THIRTEEN	1996-'97	241

THIS GAME'S THE BEST!

ONE

REDEMPTION

Die Hard Three." The headline blared across the front page of the sports section of our Seattle paper. The Seattle SuperSonics had lost a first-round playoff game at home to the Sacramento Kings, and suddenly the end of the world was near. We had been among the favorites to play for the NBA championship in each of the previous two years, but had lost in the first round of the playoffs to teams we were supposed to beat. Now everyone envisioned this happening all over again.

THIS GAME'S THE BEST!

Die Hard Three. The series was tied, one game apiece, yet everybody was abandoning ship. To my surprise, there was a lot of nervousness on our team. I don't think I've ever seen veterans react to a loss the way they did. I could see the doubt in their eyes. Athletes usually have the ability to hide their doubts. You can see it only if you study their body language or their lack of eye contact. But our guys were noticeably apprehensive, so much that so that the mood worried even me. I tried to keep everything cool in the locker room and worked to send everyone home in the right frame of mind.

Then I went home myself and had to face my son, Coby. It was a five o'clock game, so it was over by mid-evening. That gave him some time to let it sink in. Coby just lost it. I walked out on the porch to find him crying. He explained that he did not want to be in Seattle, he did not want to be a part of this, he wanted to run away to our summer home in Idaho. He sobbed, "I don't want to see you go through this again. I can't stand this."

I was shocked. Everything was so pressurized, and it indicated how I had to react. I could not go into the locker room the next day and yell at my players. I could not go in there and tell them they were worthless. I had to be different. I must say, in my career

---

REDEMPTION

I don't remember any two better days, when my mind was as sharp as it could be. I just walked in and said, "I watched the film. Gentlemen, you don't play bad basketball games, but you played a bad basketball game against Sacramento. You may have played only five or six bad games all year long, and you played a bad basketball game. You're not going to play a bad basketball game again, and I don't think Sacramento can beat you unless you play a bad basketball game. The classy thing to do now is not to go down to Sacramento and win one game as your goal, but to go down there and win both of them. Show the league that, hey, it's okay, we're in charge here."

Our reaction to that situation was indicative of our entire play-off experience last year. We did something special in every series.

Game Three was an easy game to coach—and at the same time a very hard one. It was easy because I knew what I had to do, and that was to stay calm and keep the players believing. It was hard because, frankly, believing was difficult to do at that moment. For two days after we lost Game Two everyone was abusing us. So I had to say all the things right in the pregame, all the things right in the shoot around, all the things right in the practice. It was going well, I thought, until the game started and Sacramento was playing so well. I had been afraid of that because with their home-court advantage and a huge crowd, I felt they could embarrass us. I wondered if we'd keep believing. We did—even when we were down eight points with six minutes to go in the game. That crowd was wild. The ARCO Arena is one of the hardest buildings to play basketball in because the Kings' fans are so loud. They were especially loud right then because this situation was intense. Then Frank Brickowski made a three-pointer, Sam Perkins made another, Shawn Kemp played great down the stretch, and we won the game. After we hit those clutch threes and finished that game, I knew it was the beginning of the end for Sacramento. And it was a new beginning for us.

It was fantastic. I think that was the final piece of the puzzle; now this team was going to believe in one another because we had crumbled in many other situations. The monkey was finally jumping off our backs . . . and we gladly killed the bastard. In my five years in Seattle, I can't think of a bigger win than Game Three in Sacramento.

The only situation that's even close might be when we were down two games to one in a five-game series, playing Game Four in Utah three years earlier. It was my second year with the Sonics, the year we went to the finals of the Western Conference and lost in seven. Before the game, the Jazz's Frank Layden said, "Congratulations on a great year." He was basically telling me our season was over. I walked down to our locker room and reported the exchange to our players, who used it as motivation and went out determined to win that game. Layden heard about it later and was upset with me because I had used that in the locker room. But, hey, if he didn't want it used for motivation, he shouldn't have said it. We won that game against Utah and came home for Game Five. At halftime of Game Five we were down thirteen points, but we pulled it out to win the series. Layden did not have anything to say to me then. We've patched up our relationship, although I have always felt Frank gave me just the tool I needed at the time to get my players motivated.

Once we went on to win Game Four in Sacramento and end the series, the relief was immense. Waiting for us was Houston, the defending NBA champions. But there was almost a coolness about us then. It helped that we hadn't lost to the Rockets in two years. For two years, under our breath, we had always said the Western Conference was a matchup conference. We had played Houston well, Houston had played the Phoenix Suns well, Phoenix had played us well. Even though Houston had won two consecutive NBA championships, I think we felt they were not that much better than we were, except they got the matchups in the playoffs that allowed them to win two titles.

Game Two of that series with the Rockets might have been the best game in the NBA all year long. We made thirteen consecutive three-point shots, twenty-three total, and Houston made nineteen. It was an unbelievable shoot-out. They gave us a big shock, playing us much better than they had in recent games. We won only because we made some shots we shouldn't have made. A bunch of the threes we hit were not good shot selections. But we had a momentum going, and we kept shooting the ball.

THIS GAME'S THE BEST!

The end of Game Three in that Houston series was a special moment. I had taken Coby along with the team down to Texas for that game, and the buzzer had barely sounded when he ran and jumped into my arms. What a difference a week makes. It was a really good lesson for coaches. Our world is possessed by our winning and losing. I never wanted Coby to be affected by my career. My career is hard enough on me. But then the good of the game came through too, and my son was able to experience it. He got a look at the closeness and togetherness that comes from a team working hard together and fighting together, and persevering and overcoming. He saw us humbled in one period of time but then growing and directing our future. I hope all that registered with him.

Once we won Game Three, we knew we were going to win that series. In fact, before Game Three on Houston television, Coby predicted a sweep. I had been talking to my players about keeping their mouths shut, telling them not to say anything. Then we were watching TV and saw Coby being interviewed and predicting a sweep. I almost killed him.

But he was right. We went out and beat the champions, four–nothing. We swept the champions!

Houston had won the previous two NBA titles. However, now it was a different team. In 1994 and 1995, the Rockets had fought through injuries and problems. Their veterans Hakeem Olajuwon and Clyde Drexler, who had been recently traded to Houston, had led a cast of solid role players. But last year it was as if they just did not have enough energy to overcome their obstacles. They started the playoffs strong by beating the Los Angeles Lakers, but I think in the end they knew the effort it would take to win it all and, subconsciously, I think they just did not have enough to give, a third year in a row.

Momentum seemed to be with us as we moved on to Utah, a series in which, I'm embarrassed to say, we lost our killer instinct. We blew an opportunity to make it a short series by losing Game Three. After that game I had a funny experience at dinner with some good friends, including University of Utah coach Rick Majerus. I gave the waiter my Sonics credit card to pay for the meal. A few minutes later the waiter came back a little red-faced and tried to whisper something in my ear. I told him not to whisper, that we were all friends. He then blurted out that my card was no good, which led to some good-natured ribbing about the Sonics already making plans for a new coach after a tough loss. Fortunately, it was nothing more than a computer error, and my assistant Terry Stotts's card still worked!

We went on and won Game Four in Utah, to give us a three-games-to-one lead. Then we celebrated too early. And Utah, led by John Stockton, Karl Malone, and Jeff Hornacek, showed their strength by winning a very tough game in Seattle.

Then they evened the series by winning Game Six in Utah. Of course, they did not just win that Game Six. They destroyed us by thirty-five points on national television. It was one of the few times in my life I was actually happy we had been beaten badly, because I knew we could forget about it. We knew Utah was not thirty-five points better. If we had lost a close game or choked or given away a big lead, our confidence could have been destroyed. I knew two things heading into Game Seven: Utah wasn't a lot better than us and the crowd was going to be loud and *on our side*.

What should have been a four–one series for us suddenly became one of the best series played in 1996. Not only did it go to the seventh game, but two very good basketball teams battled down to the last two minutes of the seventh game before Shawn Kemp showed why he's an All-Star. We won that series and Game Seven because Shawn won his matchup with Utah's All-Star, Karl Malone. In previous games against Utah, we'd shied away from that matchup because Karl had made the best of it. But on that day, Shawn was in a class of his own. We pulled away at the end and finally could really celebrate: We were going to the NBA Finals!

There are some people who feel that if we had won that series in a shorter period of time, our energy level would have been better for the Chicago series. Truthfully, I've wondered about it myself.

As a coach I don't ever prepare for the next opponent until we get there. But we had hired Brendon Malone to work with Dwane Casey in scouting Chicago. In fact, we had Brendon scouting the Bulls for two series, tracking their tendencies. We thought he was perfect for the job, having coached in Detroit. With the Pistons he saw Chicago a lot more often than we did. Besides, Brendon's a hell of a coach, which I think he proved as the head man in Toronto during the '95–'96 season. Brendon got screwed by the system. He did a top-ten coaching job in the NBA and was fired. But he and management did not get along because he wanted to play veterans and win immediately, while management was willing to play younger players and take losses. It bothers me when that happens to coaches, because I've been there.

Brendon was really taken by Chicago's amazing defense. I think the most intimidating time in basketball is when you can't score and, worse, you don't know how to score. You are just searching, and things that have worked with every other team suddenly don't work now. It is humiliating when, as five players, you can't figure out how to get a little ball into the basket. On the other side, great defensive teams gain so much confidence because they can sense how hard you're trying just to score a single basket. That's Chicago. So when Gary Payton was quoted as saying we were intimidated by Chicago, that's what he meant. At times, we lost confidence in our ability to score.

While Brendon was focusing on the Bulls' on-court performance, I was more struck by their team mental toughness.

I told my assistants that the Bulls' mental toughness was almost like that of the premiere teams of the '80s, not the teams of the '90s. That mental toughness was where I knew they had the edge. They learned their toughness from the Pistons and the Lakers and Boston Celtics. In my opinion they're really the only team left from the '80s era of the NBA, when players never let up, when every possession was a war. The playoffs are so much more mental than the regular season. The physical talent is more evenly balanced in the playoffs, so the difference is your team's willingness to do the dirty work, earn the extra possessions through hustle.

I decided that the mental aspect was going to be the focus of my attention in our first team meeting heading into the finals. I told our team we needed to tell the Bulls to shove it—we're going to fight you and we don't care who you are or what you've done. The sooner we did that, the better it would be for all of us.

I knew we could not win until we made this an "F_ _ _ You" series, until we *believed* we could play with them and weren't intimidated by them. So I called everyone together. I told the team we needed, as quickly as possible, to turn this into an "Up Yours" series. I wanted them to knock people on their asses and not help them up. For us to win, we felt we had to do the dirty work—go harder for rebounds, dive for every loose ball—and be the aggressor.

I wanted them to open Game One with a business-only approach. I suggested to Sam Perkins, who went to college with Michael Jordan, that I did not want him to have dinner with Michael when we were in Chicago, which Sam usually does. I said, "Sam, I don't think it's time for you to be friendly with this guy. I think Michael uses that friendliness against you." In the previous series, between the Bulls and the Orlando Magic, Michael had said he was worried in the first game when Shaquille O'Neal knocked him down. But Michael said he stopped worrying when Shaq picked him back up. Michael knew Shaq wasn't mentally tough enough.

I told my own son, Coby, that he wasn't to ask Michael for sweatbands and shoes, which he usually does. I don't think it looks good for me when my son is running around in Chicago's locker room high-fiving Michael Jordan.

The team knew I have a good-fellow North Carolina Tar Heel relationship with Michael. We've played golf together. But I told the players that none of that mattered to me. When we walked out for Game One, I was going to acknowledge Michael, shake his hand, wish him luck, but not talk to him again until the series was over. That was my contribution to developing that "Up Yours" attitude. No smiles, no friendship. I'm thinking I'm giving everyone this macho toughness, building the competitive spirit. I'm thinking I'm establishing the attitude that's necessary to really be serious about a seven-game series that is going to be physical.

Well, we walked out for Game One, and I was ready to set my example. I saw Michael, and I waited for the right time to shake his hand. He never acknowledged me. He never even said hello.

THIS GAME'S THE BEST!

He did not say hello the whole series. He was tougher than even I had planned to be. He one-upped my "Up Yours" game plan. He was all business. All business. I think everyone on our team saw that, and Michael won. He intimidated us all. There's no question in his mind that that incident had something to do with our poor start in the series.

That's what makes Michael Jordan so special. He's not only the most physically gifted athlete in the game, he's also the most fundamental player and he has the toughest mind in the game. Michael Jordan is a great talent, and everybody wants to talk about his dunking and his moves. He's an animal as a competitor, and he never dies. You might beat him, you might stop him, you might cover him, you might hit him, but he never stops playing. And to beat that guy you've got to cut his heart out. There aren't many in the league who are even close to that tough. But of those who are, two of them play on our team—Shawn Kemp and Gary Payton.

The series started out with a thud. We came to Chicago flat and could not shoot the ball worth a damn. The Bulls were ready and rested, and they thumped us good, winning by seventeen in Game One. We made it a little more respectable in Game Two yet still lost, 92–88. In those two games I believe we played more minutes of better basketball than Chicago did. But they had their two six-minute runs that were dominating—so dominating that they built large leads and then coasted. I did not feel so bad at the time because we just had not shot the ball well in those games, even though we're a decent shooting team. There's a theory that you don't win on the road in the NBA unless you shoot really well. Close, low-scoring defensive games seem to go to the home team. So I did not worry too much about those losses. Besides, we were heading home, and we had played great in Seattle all year long.

Then we proceeded to play the worst half of basketball I'd seen from our team in a long time. Jordan had scored twenty-eight points . . . at the half. Truthfully, we were a little awed. I think there were a number of us who wondered if we could beat these guys at all. We thought we were coming home and the crowd would lift us. But in the first ten minutes of the game, Chicago was up twenty-two and the crowd was gone. Everyone knew how important that game was—that if we lost it, the series was going to end quickly. But on that night the Bulls were a freight train we could not stop. They ended up winning 108–86, a humiliating blowout.

I made a coaching mistake from the start of the Chicago series. We did not go nose to nose with Jordan. We knew that Gary Payton on Jordan was the best matchup. That's one of the best matchups in the NBA—the league's scoring champion against its Defensive Player of the Year. But Gary already has to play forty minutes a game for us at point guard. I made the decision that we could not afford to tire Gary out by having him defend

THIS GAME'S THE BEST!

Jordan in addition to running our offense. And Chicago decided not to put Jordan on Gary when we were on offense. Well, that allowed Chicago to assign Ron Harper to Gary, riding him hard when we had the ball. This meant Jordan did not have to work as much on the defensive end, saving all his energy for offense. Jordan was covering Vincent Askew and Hersey Hawkins, usually our fourth and fifth offensive options. That gave Michael the ability to be a great defender off the ball and not have to defend on the ball every possession.

So for the first three games Jordan did whatever he wanted. As we prepared for Game Four, Gary said he really wanted to defend Michael. Gary's not afraid of anybody. And what did we have to lose? We had just been beaten pretty soundly and were down three games to none, on the verge of being swept in the NBA Finals. All we had to play for was pride, because no one in America thought we could even win a game. We made the switch, and it was incredible. Jordan had to work much harder for his shots, and it seemed Gary was energized by the challenge. To make matters better, Game Four was the first time we had a healthy Nate McMillan with us. He's a spiritual leader of sorts. He gave us a great lift and hit a couple of big shots.

We got a little motivation, too, from watching what was going on around us as the arena was being readied for Game Four. It was obvious that everyone was planning on us losing and ending the series. We were in the locker room when someone from our

---

REDEMPTION

----

public-relations department told me that President Clinton planned on calling after the game to congratulate both teams, which always happens *after the final game*. They wanted to know where I wanted to take the phone call. The NBA representative asked someone to tell me to keep my team on the court if the Bulls won, to be a good sport and congratulate them.

I'm sorry, I can't handle that. I was very abrupt. I told our PR folks they could stick the phone up their asses. I had no desire to talk to the president under those circumstances, even though I'm a good Democrat. I did not want to talk to anyone. We knew the NBA staff was already rehearsing the ceremony of giving out the championship trophy—before the game was played! We knew that Michael Jordan was so unconcerned he was out playing thirty-six holes of golf the day before Game Four. We knew where he played. We kept all that in the locker room because, to be honest with you, we knew we had no right to say anything. We were down three–nothing and had gone through a couple of years of being humbled. We had no right to talk. But we did have a right to get mad. We could think of ourselves as protecting the honor of the game—and the only way to do that would be to win that game.

I've always had a pet peeve about arrogance. Anyone who is successful in our sport is very cocky, confident. But I really don't think the game of basketball needs arrogance. And I think sometimes the success and money in our game, the celebrity status in

----

it, all combine to create arrogance, and that makes it difficult to handle. It motivates me more than anything else. I love playing against coaches who think they're brilliant. It annoyed me, the arrogance of some of the Chicago players. The arrogance of their staff, thinking they are geniuses. There's no genius in coaching. There are motivators and there are guys who get a little more lucky, but no geniuses. The game doesn't have any sophistication to it. It's man on man. It's body to body. It's five against five. It's each team against the other.

As you can tell, the players and I got a little fired up by that combination of things, which led to a little turnaround. We came out in Game Four and blistered the Bulls. They had beaten us by twenty-two points in Game Three—and we turned it around and won by twenty-one in Game Four. The shame is that we could never recover from being down three games to none. It wasn't realistic at that point to believe we could win four games and the series, especially the way we had been playing. Late in Game Five it was close, and I wondered if our guys would just say to themselves that they had given it a great run and relax. They did not. We won and sent the series back to Chicago for Game Six. I think that showed incredible class. We made it a good fight.

During Game Six in Chicago, we lost Nate McMillan again. He got hurt early in the second quarter. And Vincent Askew had really let me down: He blew off a team practice. Vincent and I had a long relationship dating back to our days together in the Continental Basketball Association, when we'd both been striving to get back to the NBA. That made his actions all the more difficult to handle. He was mad because he felt he wasn't getting enough playing time. With the whole season on the line, he let his entire team down. It was inexcusable. The truth is, he bailed on the team. I don't regret for a moment sitting him, disciplining him, even though our team needed all the bodies it could get. You can't coach the rest of the team if you play a guy who misses practices. No one would have respected me. If I had played Vinnie in the finals, I'd have lost the rest of the team somewhere along the way. I felt terrible, but when Vinnie came back after missing the practice, I really had only two words for him: "It's over." Those are the last two words I said to my onetime close friend. "It's over." Vincent Askew was traded after the season.

By Game Six, I saw that both teams were dead tired. I could not believe how physically exhausted everyone was. Chicago had a ten-point lead in the third quarter, and I could see we just did not have it left in the tank to win. We never got within reach, and a lot of that was because we did not have enough energy. I don't know if that was my fault or if we just got too nicked up. Maybe in the previous two games they were stronger, or maybe they were just doing a better job of feeding off the crowd, using their home-court advantage. I truly believe the home court gives you an extra 10 percent of energy, strictly from the crowd. What-ever the cause, Chicago pulled ahead and won by twelve points, 87–75. The series was over, and so was our season.

A big wild card during the finals was Chicago's forward Dennis Rodman. I do mean wild. We had the chance to pick up Dennis when he left the San Antonio Spurs for Chicago. Dennis is a good player, and I advocated signing him, but ownership made a busi-ness decision not to pick him up. Ironically, he would make the difference for the Bulls.

I think that for all of their offensive talent, Rodman was di-rectly responsible for two of the Bulls' wins in the finals. He won Game Two just by flopping every time our Frank Brickowski came near him. The referees were giving him the calls, so he would flaunt it. He would almost laugh in the face of America and say, "Hey, I tricked them again." I was asking the referees why they respected that, why they were basically respecting a cute cheater. Deep down inside I think Dennis doesn't really want to cheat the game like that, but he learned it from the best—Bill Laimbeer, formerly of the Pistons. Everybody said Laimbeer cheapened the game, and I thought Dennis was doing the same. Both Laimbeer and Rodman are great players, and they don't need to cheapen the game.

It's not necessary unless they're catering to the fans who are watching our game only because they've stopped channel surfing on their way to World Championship Wrestling. If Dennis Rodman did this stuff on the playground, you'd punch him. But you can't do that in the NBA, because the league now has so many strict regulations against fighting that you're going to hurt your team by standing up to him. Rodman knows that, and he is just begging you to deck him. He becomes a great mental as well as physical distraction. Dennis Rodman wants you to punch him. Dennis Rodman will gladly let you punch him right in the mouth and get a three-game suspension in any seven-game series. He'll do that to anybody in basketball because he's doing his job. That's his contribution to his team, and it's a huge one. He is using the rules to his advantage.

It's funny because, on the one hand, I respect him for figuring out he can make millions with that contribution. And I'd love to have him on my team. I'm not going to deny that I respect anybody who is cute enough to use the rules to his advantage. I think that shows he's a clever player. But on the other hand, he drives me nuts because of what I think he's doing to the game.

Despite what people have said, I did not send Frank Brickowski into those games to rough Dennis up. But I did tell all of our players not to let the Bulls physically intimidate them. Brick just took it a little strongly. I've never told a player to go hit another player. I have told players, "You're too soft and won't ever play if you play like that." But I've never told a guy to go hit someone. Now Brick knows his talents. His talents aren't a lot of skilled things. His value is in his body, his physicality, his anger, his toughness. He's not afraid. Putting him on Rodman was like tossing gas on fire. Rodman tries to scare you more than he tries to beat you. Brick did not back down. The end result was that Brick got tossed from two games and Dennis whipped us good. I thought Brick got nailed unjustly by the referees because he stood up to Rodman, and people were perceiving that Brick was our hatchet man. That hurt, because we needed Brickowski to play for us.

It was my mistake to take on Rodman in the press, telling reporters that I think he cheats. But I thought his antics should be discussed and be a focal point, because it seems the league, which is constantly challenged by him, is a part of his circus. I think the league should be stronger in controlling his antics. By not doing so, it has allowed him to become a national celebrity for being a freak on the court. Maybe his recent suspension for kicking a courtside cameraman will change things. Let's be honest: His antics are disruptive. His antics are confusing. His antics seem, at times, out of control. But I believe he is in control, he does know what he is doing, and he knows he can handle the chaos. He's the only one who can handle the chaos he creates. Thus, what I did was help him have more of an influence in the playoffs. I screwed up. Then he delivered two fantastic rebounding games, which were a key reason the Bulls won the championship series.

By griping to the press about Dennis, I think I fired him up.

REDEMPTION

I probably should've picked on Steve Kerr or Bill Wennington! Dennis played great in those two games—Game Two and Game Six. I mean, he had twenty rebounds, he was fantastic. Those two games were the ones that broke our heart. He was as much a part of winning those games as the Bulls' overall defense or Michael Jordan and their offense.

Late in Game Five, Dennis came up to me and asked why I was saying all that about him. I told him I said it because I believe it. I said, "I think you're acting like an ass, and I'll continue to say these things and stand up for my team all night long against you. I'm not afraid of you."

He smiled and just looked at me and asked, "Well, are we still friends when it's over?"

I said, "Probably."

I would love to have Dennis Rodman on my basketball team if I only had to manage his game. Now managing some of this other stuff and what he brings to your team atmosphere and attitude—I don't know if I could handle that. But again, I think Dennis is a little calmer than he portrays himself or is perceived to be. I think Dennis probably is a pretty cool guy.

A lot of lessons were made clear during that run through the playoffs, not the least of which was the need for team chemistry, a term not often used in the NBA. We were successful last year because of chemistry and bonding. I admitted last year that I had forgotten about chemistry. Having come from North Carolina,

THIS GAME'S THE BEST!

I'm ashamed that I had forgotten how chemistry and pieces fitting together could make a moment and a team special. Last year reminded me of all that. It was a number of little things, like Hersey Hawkins coming in and taking the edge off of everybody's playing time, that made everyone happy. That doesn't sound like much, but when you're talking about chemistry, things like that can be just what the doctor ordered.

There was a jovial nature to last year's team that was special too. Frank Brickowski always seemed to pull the right prank at the right time. Everyone enjoyed laughing. We went out bowling together. We flew together as a team to the Super Bowl, where I arranged for tickets for all the players. We had parties together, which we had never done before.

There are always between four and eight teams that have the talent to win it all in the NBA. Unless they have that special team chemistry, most of them destroy themselves as the year goes on. Former San Francisco 49ers coach Bill Walsh told me once that there are only three or four NFL teams each year that can survive the season organizationally—they don't crumble from within—and be able to win a Super Bowl. That's also true in the NBA.

We were successful, too, because of the spirit of our fans. We were 38–3 on our home court, one of the three or four best home-court records in the history of the league. Our building became an unbelievably difficult place for visiting teams to play in. The fans of Seattle had Mariner fever left over from the 1995 baseball playoff victory over the Yankees, and they transferred it to the Sonics. This city had a roll to it that I'll always remember. The fans pushed us when we needed to be pushed. The emotion was strong. It was really special.

As coaches we felt we did a solid job in the finals last year. That may sound vain, but as I look at all we *did not* know, we have to feel good about what we accomplished. I don't know if we understood, as my players did not understand, how fortunate we were to be able to play in that championship series. Even given the experience we suffered in the previous two years—the upset losses—I don't think we ever realized how great that moment in the championship was until it passed.

What you learn in the finals can never be taught, written in a book or told to a player. You have to simply live it. It is so much more intense than any other NBA experience. Everything is magnified. The pain is much more sharp. The joy is more extreme. Your mind has to be more alert, because it is tougher to find the secret or the little trick you need in order to win. You've got the best playing against the best, you've got the best coaching against the best, and there is a lot of camouflage out there. By that I mean that while every team has weaknesses, teams that make it that far are better able to hide them. That makes exploiting them even harder. So much of an NBA game is won or lost on just simple matchups and getting players where you want them to go. On a good team like Seattle we have a luxury because we have

THIS GAME'S THE BEST!

----

four or five favorable matchups—situations where we think our players are better than their players most of the time. Plus, we have versatility at the defensive end of the court. That allows us great confidence in most situations. It means I usually can push a couple of buttons and we're in fine shape. But when you play against a great team, you're pushing seven or eight buttons and it's still not a sure thing.

With the "Die Hard Three" headlines erased and the choker label gone, I'm hoping the day is near when we take that final step. History shows that teams who win championships in this league do so after getting there, learning . . . and losing. We did all three! I think Nate McMillan put it well when he said that once you get there you understand it's a little easier than you thought it was going to be and now you know what you have to do. You know what you have to concentrate on.

Personally, I'd like to win it because for the last eight years now, I've coached some of the best teams in whatever league I was in. And each time my teams did not win it all. Trying to become champion has become, I'll admit, a little frustrating. Over that period my teams have won a lot of games. But what's the difference between a winner and a champion? I want to be able

----

to tell the players, but I'm not sure I know the answer yet. I'm not sure there's a great difference. I think a lot of it comes down to confidence and the ability to react in a positive way through tough times. On that account, we should be well schooled given the hells we've gone through.

Truthfully, it gnaws at me that I haven't had a team win championships. But I remind myself that there are some great players who have never won championships. There are some great coaches who have never won championships. The perception is you can't be called a great player or a great coach unless you win a championship. I personally don't believe that. But in this business you learn to fight perception.

There is one difference I've already noticed about ending your season in the NBA Finals. It is how you wake up each day during the summer. Before this last season, I woke up each summer morning in fear, wondering what was going to happen the next season. This last summer, I woke up every day excited. I was looking forward to the '96–'97 season. I woke up looking forward to that first game, looking forward to the fans.

I was even looking forward to reading the newspaper headlines again.

TWO

A BOY FROM PITTSBURGH

I wasn't always a basketball junkie. As a boy growing up in Swissvale, Pennsylvania, I was drawn more to baseball. It was the lure of the Pittsburgh Pirates that did it to me. How could you not love the Pirates? Roberto Clemente, Bill Virdon, Dick Groat, Dick Stuart, Bob Skinner, Don Hoak, Hal Smith, Bill Mazeroski, and pitchers Bob Friend, Vern Law, Vinegar Bend Mizell, and Harvey Haddix. I could name them by position, by batting order, probably even by batting average.

THIS GAME'S THE BEST!

I was a shortstop—where else would you want to be but right in the middle of the action?—and loved hitting. But while baseball was my early passion, I learned as I was growing up that there was something wonderfully confrontational about basketball. All you had to find was one other guy to play against and you had a game. Plus, it was a team sport that allowed you to go head-to-head against another guy at the same time.

Finding kids to play with was seldom a problem in Swissvale. In our neighborhood you had a real choice of games: You had stickball and you had handball, you had baseball, you had basketball and you had wall ball. We were always out in the street playing with some kind of ball. Swissvale was filled with tall, skinny row houses. It was a lower–middle-class neighborhood with plenty of kids, plenty of alleys and plenty of walls. I threw balls at all of them.

My grandfather worked for the railroad and was home by two o'clock in the afternoon. He would be there when I got home from school. He was always encouraging me to go play. Especially baseball. He loved baseball. He had been a good athlete and a pretty fair baseball player. If there weren't any other kids around, he was right out there with me. He always made me throw the ball against the wall, which was no problem in our little neighborhood.

When I was in fourth grade my grandfather died. My father, who really hadn't shown a lot of interest in my passion for sports, stepped right in where my grandfather had been. Dad came to me then and said, "I will do everything Grandpa did for you." It was a big moment for both of us, because I knew Dad wasn't very athletic. So his efforts to make me better were hard on him. I remember playing catch with my dad and bruising his legs a lot because he was not very good at it.

Dad said he'd play with me as long as I never complained or made excuses. He was only going to commit if I fully committed. I don't think he understood athletics enough to do it any other way. In truth, that attitude—no excuses—was the best thing that ever happened to me. Today's parents sit on the sidelines and provide excuses for kids, telling them, "Your coach is screwing up," or something like that. How can we ruin our children like that?

Anyway, I think my personality comes more from my mother. She gave me my aggressiveness, my toughness. My mother was a tough woman. My father was more of a quiet soul of wisdom, of direction, of strength. My sister was older and kicked me around a little bit. I probably deserved it. I always tried to be in her world, and she never let me in. You know how that is with a little brother who is a pain in the ass.

Thanks to my upbringing, I feel I can be comfortable in almost every setting. The one setting I have a problem with is the boardroom, the suit-and-tie crowd. I don't want to offend the sophisticated, blue-blood ownership of our league, but that's not me.

THIS GAME'S THE BEST!

I'm just a blue-collar guy from a blue-collar background who found a niche working with people. I understand people, I read people, and I think I motivate people. Sometimes I motivate intellectually, sometimes it is competitive, sometimes it's by using trash talk. My success is because I read and feel what someone else is feeling.

I think that came from my shy nature as a kid. I sat back and watched a lot, observed others. Then when I was put on stage, I was overly obnoxious and out of control.

Some psychologists say people don't change. I say people change all the time. I think people gravitate back to their basic morals, but in our world today, you have to change, you have to listen, you have to observe. The people who don't do this usually live, as Henry David Thoreau said, "lives of quiet desperation." I've always understood that, and I've never desired a simple, basic life. I've always enjoyed being a leader, and although I think there have been many instances when I led poorly, I've always sought that role. We need our leaders to produce more leaders; our society doesn't encourage us to take responsibility, and I just can't handle that attitude.

My dad has always held an unshakable belief in me. Other people were more outspoken in their belief in me (or against me), but even if he didn't say a word, I knew Dad was there on my side. His support was important to me, because as cocky as I was, there was a real insecurity just below the surface. While my mother was the motivator who kicked my butt to do things right, my father was the one I never wanted to disappoint.

Dad was a parent of the '70s while I was growing up in the '60s. We had our chores and we were disciplined if they weren't done, but he wasn't regimented. It wasn't as if we had to have certain things done by 7 P.M. or else. He made personal responsibility a part of the drill. I can't thank him enough for those lessons.

My dad is a student of people. He knew how to work with everyone. I have an incredible respect for his style and his quiet belief in me because he gave me the support I so needed growing up. I just wish I had understood all that before I became a parent myself.

I wish I could go back and share more of the special moments of my life with my father. But since you can never really do that, it made it special when my wife, Cathy, arranged to have Dad on the bench on Father's Day last season, which also happened to be the fifth game of the NBA Finals with Chicago. He doesn't like to travel much, so he doesn't come to many games even though he lives near Seattle. So I was completely caught by surprise when I came out of the locker room to find him there.

It was a very emotional moment right there before the biggest game of my life. I had to fight back tears. That really was more important than the game, and it was probably the first time in my life I wasn't ashamed to admit that. In years past, I might have been upset about disrupting my pregame planning. But not on that day, and I think the players enjoyed it.

My dad had no problem with responsibility—both his and mine. He believed I would get a scholarship to college, while I was just worried, when I was in high school, about making the varsity team. Maybe it was wishful thinking for him. I remember his nervousness about finances, because my dad did not earn a lot of money and my sister was in college ahead of me. By the time I was a high school senior my dad had already paid for three years of college for my sister, and it had put a financial bite into the family fund.

As his contribution to my basketball career, my dad said he'd go anywhere, anytime, to pick me up from practices, games, whatever. He always got out of bed, never said no to picking me up at midnight across town at a recreation center, if that's where I was.

Dad had one rule, though, that could never be broken. He said, "I will support you and I will try to help you achieve your dream of a scholarship, but no coach should ever come to me and say you're not playing hard, not working to do your best." To this day, I don't think any coach—even those I work against in the NBA—has ever said that about me.

In many ways athletics was my escape. It was what I could do well, a place where I could develop my own identity.

Shortly after my grandfather died, we moved from Swissvale

to Penn Hills, a nicer suburb about twelve miles from Pittsburgh. All of a sudden I had a yard and trees and I could play hide-and-seek and I had a block of friends and I had a little stream running through my backyard and I had a pipe I could go hide in and do stupid things. I had a great dog. I had a paper route and a bike I could ride anywhere.

Still, in my own selfish way I really did not want to leave Swissvale. And it was all about sports. I knew there was a basketball league in Swissvale that you could join—but not until fifth grade. It sounds silly now, but not getting to play in that league was one of my biggest disappointments as a kid.

But soon I learned that Penn Hills also had a league. I made the elementary school basketball team as a fifth grader. It was my first experience playing "organized basketball," though if you've ever watched elementary school kids play, *organized* is not really a word you would use. I started on my sixth-grade team as a fifth-grader at Hebron Elementary School, at the top of the hill in Penn Hills. My first coach, Mr. Bitler, really had his hands full.

After our move to Penn Hills, I became a gym rat. In the summertime you could go to the elementary school and there was always something going on—softball or basketball or Ping-Pong or some other activity. I was there from nine in the morning to six in the evening every day.

The first coach who really had an influence on my life was Roger Brobst. He was the ninth-grade basketball coach, and he was always intrigued by my desire, while I was intrigued by the way he talked about the game. I was still playing baseball. I was quarterback on the football team. I was running track. But Coach Brobst kept telling me I had something going for me in basketball.

He started inviting me to go to high school games with him. We'd travel to weekend tournaments, anything we could find. And we'd talk basketball. We'd get ice cream after the game. And talk more basketball. I loved it. I started to hang out in the gym until ten o'clock at night, and Mr. Brobst was there. That ninth-grade year we had a great team and won lots of games. We won the junior high championship for the city. To a kid like me who liked to win, it was a pretty good time.

Coach Brobst loves to tell the story about a visit I paid to his classroom one morning in ninth grade. I came in complaining about a burning and itching feeling I had between my toes. "Oh, you've probably got athlete's foot," Coach Brobst said. I quit complaining. I thought that was a compliment, an inflamed badge of honor, to have something called athlete's foot!

My best friend in basketball was the guy I would go on and play with throughout high school, Donnie Wilson. There was only one lit outdoor court in Penn Hills, and that was down at the junior high school off Duff Road. Donnie and I would play down there until ten or eleven at night sometimes during the summer, just the two of us. We'd go one-on-one, pretend that we were college or NBA players.

The one thing we did do was wear out shoes. One summer Sears Roebuck had a deal on tennis shoes: If the shoes were defective, you could bring them back and the store would give you another pair. Well, as you can imagine, twelve-hour days on an outside basketball court ruined quite a few pairs of shoes. But five times one summer I took my shoes back to Sears, and five times I got a new pair because the salespeople couldn't believe their shoes could go bad so fast.

While basketball was fun, I still paid more attention to baseball through most of my junior high and high school years. However, in my junior year, things just came together for me in basketball and at the same time fell apart in baseball. I had a bad experience with my American Legion baseball team. I got hurt and wasn't playing well and just sort of lost interest. So the summer after my junior year I really committed to playing basketball seriously. I had played varsity basketball my junior year, and we had a pretty good season, losing to a team led by Ken Griffey, Sr. (of course he was just Ken Griffey then!), in the tournament that determined the Western Pennsylvania champion. That summer, going into our senior year, we all got together and were convinced we could win a state championship if we all concentrated on the game. I made that commitment.

THIS GAME'S THE BEST!

Coach Dick Misenhelter decided that even though I was a guard, my low post skills—honed on that outdoor court playing against Donnie—were good enough that he wanted to play me down there whenever a guard had me in man-to-man defense.

We had a great season that year but lost in the finals of the Western Pennsylvania Championships to a team from Farrell. In that loss I made the first basket of the game—then was an embarrassing two for eighteen from the field the rest of the way. I guess you could not say I was shy or lacked for confidence! I choked, but showed no fear of shooting. I kept complaining to the coaches that my defender was fouling me each time I shot, but no one seemed to believe me. After the game my coach watched film of the game that showed Farrell's defender was just tapping my elbow on each shot. It wasn't enough to call, but it was enough to frustrate me. I hated the result yet loved the thought of doing the same someday in a game.

I always loved thinking about the game. It was a habit I had picked up early. I remember being in sixth grade in Penn Hills and playing for the local elementary school championships. I was guarding a friend of mine. The game was being played on the court of Penn Hills High School, which at the time was a really big deal to us. We were just eleven years old, but I had played against him often, so I knew what he could and could not do. In the championship it was a one-point game with my team ahead. My friend was dribbling the ball, and I knew he was a horrible free-throw shooter. So I just tackled him, pushed him out of bounds. I figured there was no way he could hit two free throws, so I knew we'd get the ball with the score, at worst, tied. This was all running through my head. My coach wasn't responsible.

But things turned out even better than I thought. Despite my obvious foul, the referee did not call it. So we got the ball back, they fouled us, and we won the championship. That incident taught me early that you've always got to push the line of intensity and aggressiveness because you never know what you're going to get out of the game. I actually tried to foul this guy and did not get called for it.

Some have suggested that incident was the beginning of my coaching career. The truth is, I wouldn't say I ever thought much like a coach, mostly because I was always thinking about scoring. And nothing else. In eighth grade, as it would be for the next five years, Donnie Wilson played point guard opposite me at shooting guard. All I had to do was run, and he got me the ball. We stuck together through high school, and it was super. I had games where I shot fifteen layups just because I ran hard and he got me the ball. I was a good rebounder too, and I got fouled a lot.

In high school Donnie and I were known as Ham and Eggs. You can guess which one of us was ham! I was so cocky that people used to love to take me on. We got into so many fights

THIS GAME'S THE BEST!

that during my senior year we had two games where we had to play to an empty gym after the crowd erupted and the gym had to be cleared. There were only eight teams in our conference, and that year three of the games were just big brawls—and I was, I'm now embarrassed to say, one of the instigators. There's no question I like beating people. I like winning. Then I like telling them about it. I liked raising my arms after I made a basket, letting them know I did it. I still like the nervousness of competition and then feeling cocky when I am successful. It's a very good feeling. But my behavior in my high school years just did not sit well with others.

My whole high school persona was to destroy people on the court. Win, beat them, embarrass them. I was the original Gary Payton. I was a cocky, little, mean, cheating kid. I'd grab. I'd even look for tips. I loved to go to lectures where coaches taught me little tricks like hitting a shooter's elbow, grabbing the shorts, and pulling guys down at every chance. I loved the little tricks of the game. I remember one guy did a clinic on his butt, how you can use your butt in basketball. I thought it was a great clinic. How you can box the guy out, how you can set an illegal screen, how you can stick your butt in the other guy's crotch, how you can hip check a guard coming by on a screen. One day I went to a clinic on defense, and the coach brought a kid out and he pulled the kid's jockstrap out and stepped inside it. He said, "That's where you need to be to play great D." I liked that stuff. I liked

---

the intensity of it. I love playing, I love winning, and I love to be challenged.

One thing I always did in high school that I'm ashamed to admit now: Anytime one of our big guys would get fouled at one end of the court, I'd nudge him out of the way as we walked to the other end of the court, then step in and shoot his free throws. I got caught at it only one time. I don't know why I started it. They were bad free-throw shooters, but I could not believe they kept letting me do it. No one noticed: not the refs, not our coaches, not the crowd, not even my parents. I bet I shot fifty more free throws than I deserved in my high school career by doing that. It was cheating, but I was just looking for a way to create an advantage for my team. Today I would argue that someone who did that was actually not being a good teammate, because he wasn't making his teammates become better free-throw shooters. I can assure you that wasn't what I was thinking then. I'd be livid if someone did that in a game now. Funny how perspectives change as we get a little older!

People from Pittsburgh have a real blue-collar tough-mindedness to them. I don't know why, but a lot of people you meet from western Pennsylvania have a steel-mill mentality to them, even if they had nothing to do with the steel mills. I'm a product of that world, and like a lot of us from that area, I'm very proud to say that. That pride has played a role in the way I've worked throughout my career.

THIS GAME'S THE BEST!

Part of that attitude is a love for competition. Competing has always been a kick. That is one of the reasons I so love the game. While basketball is very athletic, it also is a chess match. As a coach you see it moving slowly before you. As a player it's more fast moving, more like intellectual pinball. But in either role, I love to compete.

The one thing about getting old that bothers me is I can't compete in almost any sport anymore. Golf may be my last hurrah, and I'm not very good at that. For all that basketball has given me, I'm just glad I did not stick with baseball.

THREE

PLAYING FOR COACH

I have always been a classic over-
achiever—doing more with less talent than most of my teammates on every level. I found that if I was willing to do the dirty
work of basketball, there would always be someone out there who
wanted me.

But never in my wildest dreams as a high school player would
I have imagined that the someone might be Dean Smith, legendary coach at what I consider the most legendary of basketball
programs, that of North Carolina.

THIS GAME'S THE BEST!

My big break came during my senior year in high school when I was chosen to play in the Dapper Dan Roundball Classic in Pittsburgh. The Dapper Dan pits the best high school players in Pennsylvania against a team of all-stars from the rest of the country. As you can imagine, the Pennsylvania team did not win that often, but the talent on that floor was so great that the classic always attracted college recruiters.

Although I was all-state in Pennsylvania, Sonny Vacarro, the game's organizer, really did not want me there. He just did not think I was good enough. He had said he wanted me to play in the early evening game, which matched a bunch of lesser-talented people. But at the last minute he changed his mind and put me in the A game. He gave me the break I needed.

In the game that night I didn't think I'd play much. But suddenly I was in there against one of the most highly rated point guards in the country, Jimmy Dawson of Illinois. He was everyone's all-American, and I thought I outplayed him. It was great. I stripped him twice early and took a couple of charges from him a few minutes later. It threw off his game and sealed my reputation.

More unbelievable was that our Pennsylvania team won the game. I think at the time that the Pennsylvania all-stars had won the game only four times in the history of the classic. We won by holding the ball and slowing the game down to a stall. Sounds a lot like a Dean Smith team! Even though we won, we got booed in our own building for choosing that tactic.

PLAYING FOR COACH

Before the Dapper Dan, I hadn't even heard from North Carolina. My four schools were Iowa, Duke, Maryland, and Princeton. I did not think I would go to Princeton, mostly because my first meeting with their coach was a bomb. Princeton's legendary coach Pete Carill sat in the guidance office right across from me for thirty minutes before he figured out I was the guy he had come to recruit. I guess I did not look enough like a basketball player to grab his attention. I did not recognize him; he did not recognize me. Not a real promising start. I also kept in close touch with Pitt, who had sent a young assistant coach named Tim Grgurich over to recruit me. If the name sounds familiar, it's because I hired him nearly twenty-five years later to join our Sonics coaching staff. Talk about small world.

But everything changed after the Dapper Dan. Now I was getting calls from some bigger schools, like Kentucky.

And North Carolina.

The Dapper Dan was on a Saturday night. Monday morning, Dean Smith's longtime assistant, Bill Guthridge, was at my high school. He looked at me and said, "Would you be interested in going to Carolina?" It sounded awfully good to me. At the time I still had committed to make a visit to Duke. I figured I'd spread out the two visits and go down there twice since the schools are so close together.

From the moment North Carolina expressed an interest, my ninth-grade coach, Roger Brobst, and my high school coach, Dick

THIS GAME'S THE BEST!

Misenhelter, were pushing for me to go there. Both said it was such a classy place that they could not imagine passing on the opportunity. Those men were the greatest professional influences on me early on, so it was as if Carolina had a couple of extra recruiters working for them.

Duke, on the other hand, had their alumnus Dick Groat, National League MVP in 1960 from my beloved Pittsburgh Pirates, calling on their behalf. Talk about a tough decision!

My first meeting with Coach—that's how I still address him today—was at my home in Penn Hills. Dean Smith came and took me and my family to dinner. He had a dignity to him that was different from that of other coaches. He did not have a real aggressive personality but instead was rather low-key, which I liked. Other coaches were more like salespeople, selling themselves and their programs. I think Coach was more of a speaker for his program. It is difficult to explain how it was different from other recruiting visits, but there is no question it *was* different.

Above and beyond Carolina's reputation, the reason I went there was because of Dick DeVenzio, the all-American point guard at Duke. Sounds funny that I would credit a Dukie with the decision, but it's true.

During my visit to Duke, I had a really great time. I went out with DeVenzio, and I remember being with him late at night on a Saturday. I was flying home the next day and had to make a decision soon. DeVenzio was from Pittsburgh, so I got real comfortable with him. I asked him straight out, "If you were me, Dick, where would you go to school?"

He said, "I'd go to Carolina."

I'm sure that'll make the Dukies proud to hear that, but their all-American said he'd wished he had gone to Carolina.

Had I gone to Duke, I would have been competing against Dick because he was a point guard. At Carolina the point-guard situation was a lot more open. I probably would have ended up going to Carolina, but when Dick gave me his opinion, I knew Carolina was where I should be.

As is true in most situations, almost all the schools recruiting me were using assistant coaches to do their talking. But Coach Smith got more involved with me. Coach Smith himself seemed to really want me. When things became pretty tense at the end of the recruiting period, I asked everyone to back off and not call for a week. Coach Smith agreed. Then he made daily calls to my girlfriend, asking her what I was thinking. I was flattered, actually. It just did not seem imaginable that Coach Smith, who had just taken the Tar Heels to the 1969 Final Four, where they lost to Lew Alcindor and UCLA, was interested in me. I really pinched myself a lot during that period, but the dream never ended.

Needless to say, that Final Four team was really talented, with Larry Miller, Rusty Clark, Dick Grubar, Bill Bunting, and Charlie Scott. Now, just six months later, I was playing those guys in pickup games. Freshmen were ineligible at the time—that changed a couple of years later—and at Carolina that was just the beginning of your treatment as a second-class citizen. Freshmen weren't even allowed to step foot in the locker room with the varsity. We had to walk around the varsity locker room. Their locker room had carpet in it. Ours had cement tile. The varsity locker room had wooden stalls. We had metal stalls. My freshman year we played against the varsity maybe a half-dozen times, which I loved. It was challenging to sit there and wait for your opportunity to play three on three. At that time everybody got in shape before the official opening of training camp by playing three-on-three. But as a freshman you never got on a good team. You'd get beaten eleven to three, and then you'd have to wait another half hour before you'd get on the court again. Every once in a while, if you waited around long enough, you got to play with the good guys and win a few games. But there was no question that freshmen knew their place.

Early in my freshman year I suffered a back injury. No one was really sure how it happened. Some people believed it might have been whiplash from an automobile accident I was involved in the summer before my freshman year. Anyway, during Christmas break at home in Pittsburgh I felt some back pain. When I went back to Chapel Hill I started feeling leg pains. It probably was made worse by all-night poker games. I was diagnosed with a slipped disk, so I went to the hospital and was put into traction for about a week. After being released, I was out only about a week when the disk slipped again. It was miserable. Little did I know how much worse it would get.

My season on the freshman team had ended. My last game was against Duke University on December 22, just before I went home for Christmas. I wasn't allowed to play ball again until June. The doctors decided I needed to have surgery. Today, twenty-five years later, I still don't think our doctors have much comprehension of the back, what makes it work. So imagine how little confidence I had then.

I was depressed. I was really scared. I was fearful of losing basketball. As I was getting ready for the surgery, my dad was as worried as I've ever seen him. The night before the surgery a lot of people came to say good luck. The doctor had scared the hell out of us, telling me I had the back of a sixty-year-old man and I should never play basketball again. When my dad said good night that night, he broke down and started bawling. I had never seen that from him. That really shocked me, and made me think I might be less invincible than I believed at the time.

I was concerned, too, about what was going on around me. That freshman year was the year of the antiwar riots. I wasn't doing very well in school—my grades weren't that great. When the Kent State riots happened, our campus was closed and you had the choice of taking your classes incomplete or pass-fail. I took a lot of my courses pass-fail and did not do well.

THIS GAME'S THE BEST!

Then one day I got a letter from the university saying that my scholarship was being revoked. No one had told me anything about it. I thought I was kicked out of school. I thought I was done with basketball and the coaching staff had forgotten to say anything.

I later learned the letter was a mistake. Because of the back surgery, I was just short on hours and needed summer school. On that day I felt I did not have anything going for me. I did not have a game, and I did not have a scholarship. I was in North Carolina. The Vietnam War was taking away my friends.

But you've got to take situations like that and be positive. The injury allowed me to spend time with the coaches, learning the game. I don't believe I started *thinking* the game until then. When I got to Carolina, I was startled by how complicated the game seemed. In high school I had seen an offensive machine with a tremendous passion for the game. But I scored and that was it. I had nothing to do with defense. I don't ever remember making a defensive play in high school. I was shocked when I got to Carolina and spent the first two weeks of practice learning defensive stances. We weren't even allowed to shoot during those practices! It seemed there was nothing about my game that had anything in common with North Carolina basketball.

During my injury-forced time away from the court, Carolina assistant coaches Bill Guthridge and John Lotz took me under their wing and started including me in film-watching sessions of our opponents. It was incredible. I learned how much work went into the game. They were grading film all the time. I had no idea how you did that.

I understood then how much I still had to learn. Although, in many ways, being hurt was horrible, it was also great for me, for my development as a player and a coach.

My freshman year was the last time Carolina did not win twenty games in a regular season. They won eighteen games that year with Charlie Scott, the first black player in ACC basketball history, as their star. But Charlie graduated, so in my first year of eligibility, I took his starting position. Everybody thought I would bomb, and they were predicting UNC would have an awful year. Most polls suggested we wouldn't finish any higher than seventh in the eight-team Atlantic Coast Conference. We surprised everyone, going twenty-six and six that year and winning the NIT championship, which was really big-time back then because the NCAA Tournament took only sixteen teams.

During my sophomore year I paid a price for opening my mouth. As a joke I wrote a letter to John Roche, the all-ACC and all-American guard from South Carolina. I said things like, "I can't wait until I can play your ass, and kick your ass." The letter was never supposed to get out, but a kid I knew thought it would be funny to put it in the mail.

Well, South Carolina was ranked number one when they came to Chapel Hill—and we upset them. That only made Roche all the more pumped for the return game down in Gamecockland. In that game I got knocked to the floor while taking a charge, and while the referees were looking the other way, one of South Carolina's guys kicked me in the back a couple of times *while I was down!* It was, to say the least, a real physical game.

As proud as I am that we won the NIT at the end of my sophomore year, I was the reason we weren't in the NCAAs. At the time the only way to get into the NCAAs was to win your conference tournament. They did not have all these at-large bids you have today. But in the ACC Tournament championship game, I missed a one-and-one free-throw opportunity with eleven seconds to go, when we were up by one point against South Carolina. We would go down to the other end, tie them up, and they would score a layup with six seconds to go off the jump ball. It was an unbelievable ending, and I had choked, right there in my first ACC Tournament.

It was the lowest moment I've ever gone through. Winning the ACC tournament in North Carolina is probably more important than winning the NCAA Tournament. I had never choked like that. It was a huge game. I still remember the empty feeling in the locker room.

That team was filled with talented guys like Steve Previs, Denny Wuycik, Bill Chamberlain, and Lee Dedmon. Chamberlain, Wuycik, and Previs would all play pro ball, but, like me, none of them would ever have much of a career. I would be the best pro, and I wasn't very good.

To win the NIT, we had to beat some good teams, including Duke, in the semifinals. I held Dick DeVenzio to zero points in his final college game. Then we beat Georgia Tech in the final, which was kind of anticlimatic because we won by something like fifty points.

Winning the NIT would provide us with the momentum, the belief in ourselves, that would carry us so far the next year. Of course, it was easier to go far when we brought in players like Bob McAdoo, Carolina's only junior-college transfer, and Bobby Jones, who went on to star for years in the NBA. The only player we lost was Lee Dedmon, our senior center.

We were ranked number two in the country all year long, behind Bill Walton and UCLA, and had a great year. The big moment that year was when we won the ACC Tournament, beating Tom McMillen and his Maryland Terrapins. Tom had committed to Carolina, then switched to Maryland, so that gave us added incentive. The win sent us on the NCAA Tournament, where, in the first round of the Eastern Regional, we met South Carolina, which had just left the ACC. We beat them badly. It was sweet.

Though most fans in other conferences did not understand it at the time, winning the ACC Tournament was, for us, kind of

THIS GAME'S THE BEST!

like a mini-national championship. Against the talent in the ACC, it is an incredibly hard task to win three tough games, in three straight days.

In the finals of the Eastern Regional, we played Penn. I think I scored the first eleven points of the game, and I gave the tired signal to Coach Smith, telling him I wanted to come out. He looked at me and said, "Why would I want to take you out? You're our offense." I thought that was kind of funny. We went on to win the game. We ended up in the Final Four, where we lost to Florida State. That FSU team was loaded with players like Ron King, Reggie Royals, and Lawrence McCrary. They had two six-eleven kids who were big *and* good. Plus, they had two point guards who were faster than anyone I had played. I could not cover either of them. I saw the back of their jerseys more than I saw the front.

During my senior year we played at Duke, and the fans there showed me their ultimate respect—they mocked me. They chanted "Hot dog" whenever I touched the ball. We had played earlier at North Carolina State, and the team had a beautiful large painting of my number, twenty-two, in Carolina blue. It looked as if it was embroidered into a hot dog. It was really good-looking. I wanted to buy it, but I could not get anyone to sell it to me.

I guess they saw me as a hot dog because I had long hair, was a little cocky and a lot out of control. And they knew I loved playing for Carolina. To those schools that compete against Carolina, nothing is worse than a player who loves the school.

My senior year we added a great freshman player—Mitch Kupchak—to an already good team that included Bobby Jones and myself. Kupchak joined us in the first year that NCAA rules allowed freshmen to play varsity basketball. Everyone was talking about how good Kupchak was. Now my first couple of years at Carolina I got killed in practice. The first year, Charlie Scott just beat me silly. We would play three-on-three, and I'd lose and sit for a half hour. Lose, sit for a half hour. I hated it. They treated me like shit, and they'd foul me as hard as they could. One practice my sophomore year, Larry Brown just threw me on the ground and did not give me any respect. I thought that was kind of the thing to do: The older guys should treat the younger guys like dirt.

Well that year Kupchak was practicing well. So I came in and decided he needed to be treated like a freshman. During the first week of school his team of freshmen was almost going to beat us, and Mitch was hot. I said screw this, and he kind of threw an elbow at me, and I kind of hit him with my fist. Mitch was in shock because I not only hit him, I did not let him call a foul. I found out later that he was in the locker room after that practice talking about transferring, going home or something. He thought we were too rough. What he did not know is that I was only treating him the way I had been treated over the years. You never let freshman win. You never let them have any success. If you have to, you throw them on the ground and laugh at them. It was done to me, so I did it too.

As the season progressed, we had a great year going. Our only problem was a team called North Carolina State, in Raleigh, only twenty miles away, with David Thompson, Tom Burleson, Monty Towe, and Tim Stoddard. They were on probation for recruiting violations and could not go to the NCAA, but they went undefeated, beating us three times by a total of six points. Our losses were by two, three, and one points.

Our inability to beat NC State caused us to lose our confidence a little bit. So even though we had been playing well early, we started losing games we shouldn't have lost. We even lost a couple at home. We lost to Miami of Ohio. We lost to Virginia and Wally Walker, who today is president of the Sonics. Then we lost in the first round of the ACC Tournament, getting upset by Wake Forest. We regrouped somewhat and got to the semifinals in the NIT.

But, by Carolina standards, my senior year wasn't much of a season.

Although we won a lot of games—and lost a few—while I was at Carolina, there were many things there that transcended the Ws and Ls. There was just so much tradition and energy. It's hard to explain, but there is a mystique to being a part of it, and you're proud of it, and you want to uphold it, and you want to continue it. I don't know how Coach Smith does it, but you learn very quickly when you're in North Carolina that this is a special opportunity, and it has very little to do with the individual. It has everything to do with the school and the program and winning, and winning the right way. The best decision I ever made was going to North Carolina.

And it is Coach who holds it all together. Today the two strongest influences in my coaching and my philosophy of life are still my dad and Coach Smith.

Many people talk about the Sonics' commitment to defense, to the fact that we always lead the league in steals. That began for me at Carolina. Coach starts every practice in the defensive stance for twenty minutes. Although I did not have any comprehension of defense when I went to Carolina, by the time I left I felt the game was won and lost at that end of the court. And still do.

The commitment to being unselfish and making the extra pass and moving the ball—to the team being more valuable than the individual—is the second thing Coach Smith teaches. I still believe in this today.

The third thing he stresses is respect. Respect your teammates, respect your coaches, respect the game, respect the school, represent it well. He makes you feel as if you're in a classy situation, which breeds a classy attitude and, by extension, classy people.

And Coach taught me to love the game as he does. He loves

to talk the game. He loves to be a part of the game. You know, we still get together once a year for three or four days, all the Carolina guys, to rap about basketball, play some golf, and then rap even more about basketball. Roy Williams, Eddie Fogler, Larry Brown, and others—you never know exactly who is going to be there. There are always one or two things from those meetings that I incorporate into the philosophy of our Sonics team the next year.

At those get-togethers you realize how innovative Coach still is today. He's always looking for a change, something he can do to give him an angle. The fast break he designed years ago is now run by hundreds of colleges. We even run it with the Sonics.

I was fortunate in that I came to Carolina as a point guard. At that time, and I think it is still that way now, the point guard at Carolina called the defense on every made basket. So before every game we would have a meeting, and Coach would say, "Okay, we want sixty percent man to man, twenty percent running trap, twenty percent trap." After every basket I was responsible for calling the defense. That taught me to take care of a little part of the game plan that nobody else had to do.

I remember what Coach said before the game we lost to Florida State in the Final Four. He said this is a team we probably shouldn't press, but we pressed all year so we're not going to change it. He was right. We shouldn't have pressed them!

PLAYING FOR COACH

It is funny as you think about how a moment like that shapes your future decisions. In the Sonics' 1996 season, I had played Gary Payton against the best guard almost every night, because Gary is such a good defender. Then when we got the finals, I chose not to have him cover Michael Jordan until we were already down three games to none. I made the opposite choice of Coach Smith. I scrapped what we had done all year. It was a mistake.

What Coach Smith showed me in that situation with Florida State was that he wasn't going to back off his belief in his team, even if he ran into one of the five or six teams in the country at that time that could handle our pressure. He knew it, instinctively. But by sticking to the plan, he told us he believed in us. We returned that belief in him . . . it just did not end up as a win. That's one of the things that is missing from the game today—the blind trust between a player and coach.

Coach Smith kept us believing, even when we probably shouldn't have kept our faith. Sometimes just believing resulted in miracles. Probably the greatest thing about Coach Smith's coaching is his comebacks. He has had unbelievable comebacks under impossibly difficult situations. Down seven with eight seconds to go, Carolina wins the game. Down twenty-two with fourteen minutes to go, Carolina wins the game. It's not Xs and Os. It's just belief. It's hard to be in today's pressure-filled world of sports and trust one another. It's easier to blame. It's easier to give excuses. But the truth is, the game is better when you trust one another. When you lose, you lose together, and when you win, you celebrate together.

Dick Vitale calls Dean Smith the Michelangelo of college basketball. When he says that, I'm not sure he's referring to the Coach Smith that I know. Michelangelo was an interesting man because he was a painter and a sculptor, but he also studied astrology and mathematics. He was a Renaissance man. He wasn't just an artist. I think Coach is a Renaissance man, not just a coach, and he wants his players to have diverse personalities. He encourages them to spend time in basketball, but also time in their house of worship and time in academia and time in the city. When I visited Carolina, I actually had to go to a couple of lunches and dinners with professors, even the president of the university. Coach introduced us to interesting people all the time: Billy Graham, the governor of the state, and others. In the summertime, if you did not want to play basketball, he wanted you to take an intriguing trip. Some guys would go to Europe, some guys would go to Washington, D.C. Coach provided his players with the freedom to be themselves and grow. Sometimes leaders are controlling and they subtract from people's lives, whereas Coach Smith develops the skills and talents of his people.

I was lucky to have played for Coach. It is a shame that one day he'll retire. I've never been shy about saying the head coaching job at Carolina is the best basketball job in America, and only that would lead me to walk in to the Sonics general manager and ask to quit. If Coach decided to retire tomorrow and they offered me the job, I would try to go immediately. I don't think there is another job in America that I would leave the Sonics to accept. It would be such an honor that—I probably shouldn't say this—I would do it almost for nothing. I'm sure the pressure would be unbelievable. But the challenge would be unbelievable too.

I say all that as if it might happen, even though I know it is really a fantasy. There will be tremendous people wanting that job, including guys like Larry Brown and Roy Williams, and maybe Eddie Fogler. It'll probably be a bigger dogfight than a home game against Duke!

FOUR

THOSE ABA DAYS

Coming out of Carolina, my options for a future in basketball did not really seem good. The guys who were going on to star in the pros were much more talented than I was. All I was hoping for was a chance. If someone drafted me, I felt I could make it.

Well, I did not just get one chance. I got two. In 1973, I was drafted in the third round by the NBA's New York Knicks. A little later I was chosen in the fourth round by the rival American Basketball Association's Memphis Tams.

THIS GAME'S THE BEST!

Friends told me my best shot at making a team was in the ABA, so I focused my efforts there. Then the Memphis team screwed up and lost my draft rights when it failed to offer me a contract within the allotted time. I wasn't sure what was going to happen.

Within days the ABA's San Antonio Spurs offered me a three-year contract with salaries of $35,000, $40,000, and $45,000. I thought I'd hit the lottery! The Spurs made my decision easy by guaranteeing the first year of my money, something the NBA wasn't going to do.

The thing about playing back then was that only the real fans had any idea who you were. In the ABA we were almost never on television. Today if you make one great play in a college game, everyone sees it on ESPN and CNN/SI, so you're an instant celebrity. You can use it to get dates and stuff. That wasn't true with the ABA. Hell, my own wife, Cathy, whom I met when I was with the Spurs, had never heard of the team. When I told her I was a Spur, she thought I was a football player. Cathy was a flight attendant with Braniff, her best friend was dating my teammate Coby Dietrick—and she still didn't know.

The ABA was just plain more fun than the NBA. In the ABA you never knew if you were going to have a job. You played teams fifteen, sixteen times a year, and there was a lot of camaraderie. There were a lot of fights too. When you play someone that many times in a year, you have friction that often gets out of control.

THOSE ABA DAYS

It's just natural. Many times you knew before even starting the game who was going to fight. In the locker room, you'd say, "Okay, Fatty and George are going to get into it tonight," or "Shimmy and this guy are going to get into it tonight."

We had guys chase other guys out of the gym with chairs. I saw a player pull a stomach muscle trying to pick up a chair that was bolted to the floor. He was out for two weeks. There were coaches who were crazy too. I remember one game when Butch van Breda Kolff got a technical in the first quarter. There was a bar on the first floor of the Spur arena called the Spur Corral, and Butch just walked over to the bar for two quarters, then came back in the fourth.

You had some weird moments in the ABA, moments that are lost in today's NBA because the levity of the game has been taken away. Today's coaches are too damn serious. The game was made to be enjoyed, and for me the best I've ever played is when it has been fun.

It was fun in the ABA. I liked the feel of the ABA because it was a renegade league that still had good players. Go figure that I would enjoy being part of a renegade league! The NBA knew we had good players, yet they refused to accept us. They refused to respect us. We would play exhibition games against NBA teams and win twenty-two games and lose nine, every year. Still, the NBA players said that was only because we took the games more seriously than they took them. Bullshit. They always had an answer for us, which is fine because they were the king and we were Robin Hood. We were trying to steal from them.

The ABA, in my opinion, would have survived if it had managed to get a television contract and had learned to work the national media as the NBA did. But without those two things the league was doomed. Basketball people knew we played good ball, but without a TV deal, the public did not know.

The Spurs had just moved to San Antonio from Dallas, and I was the first draft choice that new owner Angelo Drossos signed. Among San Antonio fans, that made me sort of popular. Mc-Combs did not help me, though, when he told a reporter that I knew as much about basketball as the coaches did.

He said that because I was always so outspoken about our team. I think I'm a very loyal player. But I also wanted to win, and if I saw something I felt could help our team win, I had trouble keeping it in. Sometimes I did it the right way, sometimes I probably did it the wrong way. But I don't think I ever did it viciously to hurt a coach or to undermine a coach or to backstab a coach. I did it to help win. I would make suggestions, and they would end up in the paper, not sounding like what I was trying to do.

I had a lot of time for thoughts about basketball then, mostly because I wasn't playing much more than twenty minutes a game, even in my best years. When you're sitting on the bench, you have time to think about the game. And that's what I did. After games I'd look for an assistant coach to go out with so I could talk about the game more. I was analyzing pro basketball very early in my playing career, even when I was a pretty good player, but toward the end, when I tore up my knees and lost my edge, all I could do was think the game.

I probably knew I was going to become a coach even before I sat on my first ABA bench. The summer after my senior year at Carolina, I traveled to Russia with coaches Larry Brown, who was then with the Carolina Cougars, and Doug Moe and a team of U.S. all-stars. Even though I was still young, I coached, I did not play. That summer when I saw Larry work the team, watched him teach players, I knew that's what I wanted to do. It was a fun team because it was all small-college players like Foots Walker and Trent Robinson. We went over there and won four out of six games.

Larry was very energetic, much like Coach. The more I watched, the more I thought I could do that. I just felt good on the sidelines. I felt good sharing my knowledge of the game.

My first coach in the ABA was Tom Nissalke. You could not have asked for a coach more different than Dean Smith. It was like going from heaven to hell. It was totally weird. Nissalke did not like me. Nissalke, like Coach Smith, was totally structured. But Nissalke was offensively oriented, whereas Coach Smith believed the game is dictated by the defense.

Knowing that the coach did not like me, I was nervous as hell.

THIS GAME'S THE BEST!

I could not make a jump shot for the first two weeks of camp. I was awful. I think we played four exhibition games, and we were losing them all by twenty. We weren't even close. Still, I didn't play a minute. I think what he was doing was showing up the owner. The owner had signed me to a guaranteed contract, and Nissalke had not wanted to sign me. He had wanted to sign somebody else, but the owner signed me anyway. So I think it was a coach-owner conflict for a while.

We played the first five games of my first season, and nothing changed. It was nothing but pine time for me. We were getting killed, and I wasn't playing. I'm not used to losing. I'm not used to not playing. I remember staying after practice every day and shooting. I did not want to be in the locker room with the players. I was scared that my career was over, and it hadn't even begun.

Game Six was against George Gervin and the Virginia Squires. I got the call—it was the first time I was in a professional game. I scored twenty-two points and took four charges on Gervin. We won. A month later I was starting.

The next year, right in the middle of the season, we were heading toward our plane for a road trip when someone told me Nissalke had been fired. It wasn't as if we'd been bad. In fact, we had been doing well; we began the season 18–10, a good start. The general manager decided Bob Bass was going to coach the team. I was kind of pissed off because I had mended my fences and Nissalke and I were communicating. I did not know how you fired a coach that was winning, especially in the middle of the season. At that moment I realized how much of a business this was. It kind of struck me as, damn, so this is how it works. I decided to keep my head down and just play hard, hoping not to lose my job.

About the only thing I'm remembered for from my playing days was my toughness. It certainly wasn't my scoring and surely not my speed. That reputation really was made solid during an event that has become known as the Easter Day massacre.

The Spurs were in the playoffs, playing Dr. J and the New Jersey Nets, and it was a tough series. It was Game Four, we were up two games to one, and my job was basically to go in and bother Brian Taylor, the Nets point guard. I was to pick him up when he crossed half court and bump him to throw his game off. The first possession after I came into the game, which was probably the end of the first quarter, he elbowed me. I have a scar underneath my chin, and he opened it up. I looked at him, and he just turned and walked away. I knew he had hit me pretty good, but suddenly I saw blood, and I could not handle it. So I jumped him from behind. I hit him and knocked him down. Both benches just emptied, and the thing went on for about ten minutes. Actually, during the fight, Brian came back and got me again. But in between I was kicked and I was grabbed. It was probably the biggest fight I've seen on a basketball court.

The only other moment anyone remembers from my playing

THIS GAME'S THE BEST!

----

days was when six-feet-eight, 260-pound forward George Mc-
Ginnis of the Indiana Pacers knocked me into next month while
I was taking a charge. McGinnis used to call me a flea because of
the way I guarded people. I had a reputation for taking charges.
But this wasn't a real smart one.

We were ahead by seventeen points or so at the time, so basically the game was over. But all I saw was George coming toward
the basket on a fast break. I moved over instinctively to take the
charge, and he said, "I'm going to knock you out" and ran me
over. He actually picked up speed rather than trying to change
direction. There was no question he was giving me his best shot.
I was standing near the free-throw line but ended up underneath
the basket. He got my testicles really good with his foot, lifted
me up off the ground with his forearm. I was hurting. The goal
standard had foam rubber around it, and the runner had little
indentations in it. I hit the post so hard that my back and butt
were completely bruised—except for the dots where those little
holes were. I looked as if I had the imprint of that foam rubber
on my butt.

I was knocked groggy and taken out on a stretcher, but you
know that's just basketball. I took a lot of charges, some of them
hard, and some of them not so hard. The fact that we were up by
double digits did not matter, because that's what you're supposed
to do. You don't coach the game any differently when you are up
eighteen, you shouldn't play it any differently, and you shouldn't

----

referee it differently either. Even today I think I coach the same way. I'm more relaxed when we're up seventeen, but I've told coaches you only stop coaching the last minute of the game with a twenty-point lead. No other situation should allow you to stop doing what you do best.

Contrary to ABA lore, I did not start a fight with the legendary Pete Maravich . . . but I did hit him once. It was late in a game, and he elbowed me in my chin on that same scar. He just blatantly jabbed me with a punch. It was very late in the game, and I said, "You're not going to get away with this." This was when you were allowed to punch without getting suspended for many games, and I kind of just threw a punch and hit him. I don't know if he slipped or not, but he fell to the floor and I jumped on top of him, and I remember Nate Williams, all six-feet-four, 220 pounds of him, jumped on top of me. Later, when Pistol Pete died, I learned I was the only player who ever fought him in a game. I don't know if that's a positive or a negative.

I did not get physical only in games; I was equally as rowdy in practice. Just ask George Gervin. While I was with the Spurs, they bought out the contracts of Gervin and Swen Nater and added them to our team. At the time Gervin was a forward and one of the sweetest shooting players I've ever been around. But in my third year Gervin moved to guard. I was starting. Gervin took my place.

So you trivia fans should remember that NBA scoring champ

THIS GAME'S THE BEST!

George Gervin took George Karl's place in the starting lineup. I want to go down in Hall of Fame history someday. I went from playing a lot to not playing at all. Mike Gale was the guard they brought in off the bench. So all the problems my players bitch about today, about how quickly their role on a team can change— I have gone through those problems, and so I try to be a little sympathetic.

Well, when Gervin moved to guard I started playing against him every day in practice. I took it as a challenge, and Gervin wasn't a great practice guy. I would win a lot of those games. I got around him, and scored layups, and our team would win. Gervin would be just hanging out and looking at his watch, asking when practice was going to end because he did not need to practice; he was too good. Once in a while I'd make a statement in practice and kick his ass.

But then during my last couple of years in the league, when my career was really going downhill, I decided to start making other people practice harder. I did not think our team ever practiced hard enough to win championships. The only thing I could give to my team was my practices, because I wasn't playing. So I would go out there and beat the shit out of them, and it got to the point one year that Bob Bass stopped scrimmaging because there were too many fights. We were throwing elbows, taking dirty shots, knocking people on their asses, and cursing one another out. Even though I was playing as hard as I could, it was a joke. I had no chance against them, because they were so much more talented.

All my fighting—with others and with my own team—did not make much difference. The Spurs won about fifty games each year but never won a championship.

During my fifth season it was obvious I wasn't quick enough to play anymore. The point was made abundantly clear during an early game at Washington against the Bullets. I was headed downcourt for an uncontested layup when my former Carolina teammate Mitch Kupchak—the freshman I had beaten up on in practice—chased me down and blocked my shot from behind. The two of us were going to dinner that night after the game, and I told him I was hurt he hadn't been more considerate of a friend who was struggling to make a team. He reminded me of our first go-around at Carolina and made it clear that, as the saying goes, payback's a bitch.

As things were winding down for me on the court, the coaches moved me to the bench as a scout and an assistant coach. It was really a great opportunity to learn from Bob Bass and his successor Doug Moe, the coaches at the time.

About the time I moved to the bench, Cathy and I were married and we later welcomed our daughter Kelci into the world. Life was settling down for us. Then Doug Moe was fired. When the head coach goes, so do all of his assistants.

I was, for the first of several times, unemployed.

FIVE

TOWNS YOU'VE NEVER HEARD OF

I was unemployed. But not for long. During the summer of 1980, after we were all fired in San Antonio, I was in Florida playing tennis with some friends. It was a mixed-doubles match—that my team would go on to win, no doubt! The guy on the other team just happened to be Ryan Blake, son of well-known NBA scout Marty Blake. Marty was there watching when Ryan, a tennis pro for a local club, hit a hard serve my way. I dove on the concrete court to return it. I heard later that that really impressed Marty, who mentioned my name to a couple of folks. Sometimes life changes in the damnedest of places.

One of the people Marty mentioned me to was Ray Dobbs, owner of the Continental Basketball Association team in Great Falls, Montana. Dobbs called and offered me a job: head coach of the Golden Nuggets. The salary was $18,000, a lot less than I had earned as an assistant with the Spurs. But it was a job. And it was a chance to be the head man.

Actually, Ray was the second CBA owner who called our house to discuss the job. When a guy from Billings called earlier that day, I was out golfing, so first he talked to Cathy. When he said he was with a CBA team, Cathy asked him what the CBA was! We were certainly about ready to find out.

Ray invited us to come up and check out Great Falls before making our decision. Cathy pulled out an encyclopedia and looked at pictures of Montana, and it was beautiful. We did not know that most of the pictures were taken in the western part of the state, where there are glacial parks. Great Falls, on the other hand, is in central Montana, which is desertlike and desolate. It was so different from what we had expected. We arrived to find the terrain was flat, the airport was on a plateau, and the city was down below. I was expecting mountains and trees. But there are very few trees in Great Falls. And the wind blows like you wouldn't believe! *USA Today* listed Great Falls as the windiest

----

city in the United States, ahead of Chicago. It blew our fence down two or three times.

Despite the wind and the cold, I looked at the offers from Billings and Great Falls and believed the Golden Nuggets had a better chance of being a real team. It turned out to be a great decision.

The weather wasn't the only thing reminding me how far I'd traveled from the sidelines in San Antonio. The Golden Nuggets practiced in a Salvation Army gym. Our practices were usually the first event of the day in the gym, so the heat wasn't on. The balls wouldn't bounce right. The players could not get comfortable. Everything about the situation was a challenge.

At the end of our first season our owner went bankrupt, and Cathy and I ended up paying the players out of our savings. We did not want anybody to know, so we did not tell the players. We filed income taxes on eight thousand dollars that year.

But while I was worrying about player salaries, I wasn't aware that the owner wasn't paying rent for our use of the high school gym, where we played our games. He hadn't paid the rent all year. When we made the playoffs, the school board decided it was cutting us off. I had to go before the school board and negotiate a payment plan. I promised them 25 percent of the gate receipts just so they'd open the gym. I had to go up every week and beg to play in the gym.

THIS GAME'S THE BEST!

The owner left and, as scary as it may sound, we were running the team. But before he left, he made the strangest payment I've ever seen. He gave us his silverware and said if he could not work out his money problems, we could pawn it as a down payment on what was left of my salary.

Well, a second owner came in and said he'd take the silverware. He said, "I'll keep that for you and pay you. I'll just take the silverware and give you the money." He did not give us the money, and he kept the silverware. I never did see the silverware again. He snuck off to Helena, and we never saw him again.

It was tough there for a while. I was earning just $18,000 but had gotten only about $13,000 of that before the silverware incident. Then I spent about $5,000 of what I had on the players. Tough year.

But other than the financial end, which was obviously a debacle, life in the league was always exciting. Kelci, our older child, was eighteen months old when we moved to Montana. She became known as the littlest Nugget. Both Cathy and Kelci traveled with us when the team went on the road.

Unlike today's NBA travel on charter jets with private service, we went everywhere in cars and vans. I remember on the first road trip we took a Suburban and one rental car. We'd put all our bags in the back of the Suburban, and Geoff Crompton, a 310-pound teddy bear of a center, would lie down on them.

TOWNS YOU'VE NEVER HEARD OF

Cromp was so big that the company that made our uniforms could not make shorts for him. The company would send us fabric, and Cathy made the shorts for him. His waist was about fifty-four inches; his thigh was thirty-eight inches.

The first year his weight was under control—he was about three hundred pounds. He was good enough that he had guaranteed offers in the NBA if he would get down to 270 or 280. But he never could, so he always ended up playing in the CBA and was a great player. He took up a lot of room in the middle, knew how to defend, and was the last of the great screeners. Every basketball coach is looking for those skills. We drove everywhere with Cromp stretched out on the luggage.

Our trip from hell was the death-defying three-game chicken series, as we called it. Our owners had hired the famous San Diego Chicken as a promotional stunt to increase attendance. We played in Lethbridge, Canada, on a Friday night. We had to drive to Billings and play on Saturday night, and then we had a noon game in Missoula on Sunday. We had hired the chicken to be there for all three games.

The idea of a three-game chicken series grew from an event the year before. The chicken actually saved the season for the Golden Nuggets. I had met Ted Gianellis, the man behind the chicken, and asked how much he'd charge to come in and get our fans revved up. He said it would be $5,000, so I went to busi-

THIS GAME'S THE BEST!

nessmen in Great Falls and got them to sponsor the chicken. Then we had all our fans, including our season-ticket holders, buy another ticket for the chicken game. It was a huge success.

The word was out that the only way we were going to survive was if we drew four thousand fans for the chicken game. We got only about twenty-eight hundred fans, but at six dollars a head, we walked out of there with $12,000. In the CBA, $12,000 goes a long way. That's probably at least six to eight weeks of salary for the entire team.

After the success of that game, the owner said, "Why not do it next year and take him with us three times?" Thus began the three-game chicken series. But as we headed to the third game in Missoula, the humor of the situation was completely gone. On a good day the drive from Billings to Missoula takes five hours. This was not a good day. In fact, it was snowing so hard that the roads were being closed. You could not see the road. The five-hour drive took about nine hours. We left Billings after midnight because we had just played a game. We got into Missoula at ten o'clock in the morning, and we had a game to play at noon. The players got two hours of sleep before the game.

Because of the blizzard—and because the university there had played a home game the night before—we had a crowd of one hundred. It was so bad that we went out with the chicken after the game and had to renegotiate a settlement. We took him to

- -

Godfather's Pizza in Missoula and begged Ted to take $2,500 for that game because we could not pay him.

We were pretty far from the big time.

One time during a game in Alaska, we had blown a big lead on the road and, even though we were ahead, we were in danger of losing in the last minute. We had a great player in U.S. Reed, but he was getting frustrated by the defense the Anchorage team was playing. We could not get anything up. The ball went out of bounds. Out of frustration, I called time-out. I drew up this real elaborate play that would take at least ten seconds to run, probably more like fifteen seconds. As we left the huddle, we looked up at the shot clock, and only three seconds were left. I had totally forgotten to check the shot clock. We did not have assistant coaches on road games, so I had had no help.

Well, as they walked on the court, Terry Stotts and U.S. Reed made eye contact and knew what they were going to do. In Anchorage they had a fan-shaped backboard, not the standard square kind. With the fan backboard you could throw the ball kind of up over the rounded corner, right over the rim. Terry threw a perfect pass. U.S. Reed was one of the best jumpers I've ever seen, and he leaped over and dunked it. I think he got fouled. We won the game, and afterward several reporters said what a great call that was. Being modest, I took credit for it!

We had just eight players on the traveling squad and two

- -

THIS GAME'S THE BEST!

"home" players. Home players got paid only to play at home. We could not take them on the road. Usually the home players were good local athletes who maybe played small-college basketball. No way were they as good as the eight regulars.

Still, all three years in Montana one of my home players ended up starting in the finals of the CBA championship. We lost so many players to the NBA or to European teams that by year's end, the home players were among the best we had.

The great thing about the CBA was you got to see some really classy people trying to make the most of a tough situation. In my third year we had a first-rate team with Robert Smith, Terry Stotts, and John Douglas. We made it to the finals of the CBA championship. But the first round of the playoffs came while there was a players' strike being threatened in the NBA.

At the time we were tied one–one in the first-round series against Wyoming and were headed for the next three games on the road. We had already lost a couple of players to the NBA, and Wyoming was playing well. Just then, San Antonio called to say they really wanted Robert Smith, and immediately— because if the strike happened they were looking for players who would cross the picket line. They said they were getting a start on looking for guys who would fill that role.

Robert was the best player in the CBA, so it was natural that the Spurs would want to pick him up. Robert came to me and said, "George, I don't want to leave the team until the Wyoming

----

series is over. We will win the series for you, and then I'll go." I called San Antonio back and explained what Robert wanted to do. The Spurs did not like the idea, but Robert stuck to it. He did just as he had promised, and we won the next two games and the series, then he went on to the NBA. He took a risk for us, and I've always thought that was a real show of class.

Robert left, and the team was headed to the CBA Finals. So who starts in place of the league's best player? A guy named Donnie Newman. Donnie was one of our home players and earned a whopping fifty dollars per game when we played at home. We lost.

The same year, the owner got tired of us flying in guys for tryouts, because a ticket to Great Falls was at least $800 from just about anywhere. So he made us pick up players from the College of Great Falls. One of the kids we picked up, Dean McFadden, was a great shooter. Just like the year before, our two best players were called up to the NBA right before the playoffs, so there we were with Dean McFadden playing a big part in the CBA Finals in Detroit. Perhaps three thousand people might have been in the University of Detroit building.

So this kid, McFadden, came into Detroit, and they started trash talking him, knocking him on his ass, and he had an awful first game. I went to him and said, "Dean, you're going to play about nine minutes a game—four minutes in the first half, five minutes in the second half. The only thing you can do on a CBA level is shoot. So when you get in the game, just shoot it. If you force a couple, you miss a couple, I'll take your ass out and we'll be fine, but don't go in there and play scared. Just go in and shoot."

We won the next game in Detroit when McFadden made four threes and started talking trash. I was loving it. Here's a College of Great Falls kid just getting off in the middle of Detroit.

Another time our home player was actually the local television sportscaster for the station in Great Falls. He was the best player available in the city!

When we traveled, we used to take the referees with us. The referees would be in the same car. I even had two referees stay at my house. They could not afford hotels, or we'd get back so late their reservation would get canceled, so they'd ask to stay over.

Unfortunately, my hospitality did not earn me any points with the referees. I think some of them did not like me because I knew the rules better than they did. I actually protested two games and won both protests. How many protests in the history of the sport have been upheld? Not many. I protested two games in the CBA, and both of them had to be upheld.

All in all, the referees in the CBA were fine. You just have to know up front that in the CBA they are young and not very good. But what I found out when I went to the NBA is that all the CBA guys you thought were going to be your buddies would screw you because they did not want the perception of a close relationship. It was like, "We are going to show you we're not going to be partial."

One of my most memorable referee moments came while I was in Great Falls. We were down three with about thirty seconds to go when the referee made an awful call and our player got a technical for arguing the call. I called time-out, and I remember standing there thinking, Should I try to coach this team in this situation, or should I acknowledge this is not a win and just go after the referee. The referee won, and I went to the middle of the court and started clapping. "That was a hell of a call, that was one of the best basketball calls I have ever seen," I said, mocking him. As I suspected, he called a technical on me. I said, "Oh that's even better." I took my coat off, and I threw it to the side. "It's calls like that that explain why you should be in the NBA," I said. Then I took off my tie and threw it to the sidelines. The I took off my shirt. I said, "How long are you going to wait until you throw my ass out of here?" There is an unwritten rule in basketball that you don't throw a guy out at the end of the game if you can avoid it. I made it a call he could not avoid, but he let me get to the third button on my trousers before he tossed me.

I loved playing in the ABA. I love the talent of the NBA. But nothing compares to the enjoyment I had in the CBA. The CBA is a big part of George Karl—my education, my coaching beliefs in versatility, playing small and big lineups, having to change. All that grew out of life in the CBA, where you have to be ready for change because your life is always in chaos. You're in crisis management at all times. You can never get organized because you don't have enough staff; you don't have enough money to run the team professionally, so you're always piecing it together. That training has been immensely important to my work in the NBA.

The CBA also brought me a relationship with Terry Stotts, who is on our Sonics staff today as an assistant coach. Terry played for me all three years at Montana and was an assistant with me in Albany. He is, in my opinion, the Roy Williams of the NBA. Roy was the fourth assistant at Carolina for years until Dean Smith helped him get the Kansas job. Now he's one of the hottest names in the business. If you like Dean Smith basketball, you'll like Roy Williams. If you like George Karl basketball, you'll like Terry Stotts. He's got all the skills to go further than I have with this game.

So I have many things I can look at today and link directly to my experiences in the CBA. Every coach ought to have those experiences.

I think the CBA is the best league for teaching—both players and coaches. You have many players playing out of position, sizewise, and having to learn new positions. Those players really wanted to be in the NBA instead, and they're mentally defeated for the first times in their lives. As a result they're searching for answers when they come to you, and if you give them something they can use, they really warm up to you, and they can take it a long way.

I like the CBA, too, because it's the last professional league where the coach has the hammer. He has the ability to keep or can any player he wants. Nowhere else is that true.

That's why I honestly think the CBA offers the best coaching situation in any sport—because the coach has full authority to change his team. And there are no guaranteed contracts. I've traded all-league guys because I did not want to deal with their attitude. One time I took a look at a kid named Steve Burtt. He wanted to play for me, but he wanted guaranteed minutes. He wouldn't come unless we would play him thirty minutes a game. I said, screw that, man. He'll never play for me. There was another kid named Marlon Redmon when I was in Montana. I traded him to Billings because he was always late to practice. After we traded him, he probably got forty on us six times. That's okay, because he was someone else's headache.

And shaping your team in the CBA is important. The more you get the team into the game in the CBA, the more success you're going to have. That's because most players in the CBA are selfish. Well, this is true in the NBA too. I would say most NBA players have a degree of selfishness to them, but this is definitely true in the CBA. The vast majority of CBA players think their route to the NBA is numbers. They're determined to go out and get their numbers. I love playing guys who want so badly to score. You know that if you frustrate them early, they'll start forcing shots and screwing up their own team.

In the CBA, if you like a guy's heart, you can find a place on your team for him. Take Vincent Askew. Vinnie had been cut in the NBA but was really looking for a way back. So he was willing to do anything. When he came to us, he could not make an outside jump shot, so we could not play him at shooting guard. He wasn't fast enough to guard small forwards. So we tried him at power forward. He was a six-feet-four power forward. Where else in the world could you do that? You can get away with that in the CBA, and it was great, and we won big. You could not do that in the NBA.

Just getting Vinnie on the floor and getting him playing time allowed him to regain his confidence. That was my biggest job in the CBA—that and negotiating with the school board! A lot of these guys weren't sure they could play anymore. Once they got that confidence back, all kinds of other things happened that were good for them. Confidence is the key for all of us. When we have confidence, we perform better. When we have confidence, we think better. When we have confidence, we bond better, we relate better.

It's difficult to work on confidence in the NBA. I've seen the best players in basketball lose their confidence. I've seen great players shoot bricks on the free-throw line at a crucial spot in the game, when the day before they made ninety-nine out of one hundred shots. That mental toughness, that ability to maintain your confidence, is the difference between the college and the pro game.

In the CBA one of the greatest challenges is entertaining yourself in towns you've never heard of. We had contests and world records. Cromp, for example, could drink a six-pack of beer in eight minutes. Terry Stotts once said a memorable evening in Great Falls was when he and I won eighty-three free-game credits on the video game Donkey Kong. We loved to play Donkey Kong. It was simple, like us. These days the machines are too sophisticated.

The NBA, by contrast, is like today's video games. It's too serious, too sophisticated. It's gotten to the point where we can't laugh because someone is going to criticize us for not being serious enough. We can't have any levity anymore. It's sad, because the game—the competitive nature of the game—needs some release, some laughter.

After games our CBA teams sold the postgame party to restaurants and bars. We'd advertise the party for them as long as they fed our players. It was a way of saving the players a little cash. One year we did not give the players their per-diem pay because we could not afford the fifteen dollars a day. So we traded meals out at restaurants. The worst meal was breakfast. Our breakfast sponsor was Dairy Queen, which was a block from the practice facility, and so our guys had two-dollar vouchers to go to the Dairy Queen and get an egg sandwich.

The players practically lived with my family and me at our house. We'd always have guys over for dinner, including at Thanksgiving and Christmas. Cathy would cook, and I know the players loved the free food. (The truth is, I think they came over because we had cable.) Not only did you have to have a practice plan in the CBA, you had to have a meal plan, because after practice the first point of discussion was where everyone was going to eat that day, and then the next day, and the day after that.

But as great as the CBA is, I don't think its potential has ever been tapped. I would love to see the CBA developed as a true minor league, because I believe it would help coaches, players, and referees too. I think it would help the game. Unfortunately, there are too many special interests who are keeping that from happening. I have heard that neither the NBA owners nor the Players Association wants it. But I think the true basketball people want it, and they would like to see it happen soon.

If the CBA were an NBA minor league, imagine how great it would be for coaches who have grown tired of the stresses of the NBA to go to Great Falls and just coach. They could go down to the CBA and maybe have a couple of good years, rebuild their confidence. I think it'd be great.

The CBA really allowed me to get the most out of my competitive nature. It is the perfect place for a guy who likes to push the game rather than react to it. It is a great place for a coach who loves to look for an advantage. I like to get into a game, looking for an angle where I feel I can win. I don't like to play the Ping-Pong game of coaching where everything your opponent does, you counter. I like taking chances more than sitting back. I would rather play some cards and try to create opportunities rather than just allow the game to happen, because I think when you sit back and watch, it sometimes doesn't happen the way you'd like. The more talented your team, the more you can sit back and say, hey, we're okay, we will figure it out. The less talented you are, the more aggressive you need to be. Our teams were always marginally talented.

Michael Cage, one of my first Sonics players, once said it was "Looney Tunes" playing for me, because he felt I was always in a constant game of dare with the opposing coach. I'll agree with that. I don't mind my opponent knowing I'll try any mismatch if I think it is where my team has an advantage. Sometimes I'll post up my point guard if that's the matchup most to our advantage. Michael was being funny, but I'm not the only coach who does that. Don Nelson was famous for it.

Today's CBA is a far cry from the league I joined in the early 1980s. I mean, now the players make good money. Today there are CBA players earning $2,000 a week, $50,000 a year. My last year in the CBA, when we were 50–6, we paid everybody the exact same amount of money. I told their agents, Your client is not coming here to make money. He's coming here to get the hell out of here. I said, We're going to take what our salary cap is and divide it by ten, and that's what your player is going to make. I think my owner paid a few guys under the table, but I don't know. I heard he did. To get Vincent Askew back from Italy, where he was making about $150,000 a year, I think Vinnie might have been paid something. I never asked him because I don't want to know.

The funny thing about the CBA is that the team that is best at the beginning of the year is seldom the best at the end of the year. By season's end you'll usually find the top 10 percent of the players have gone to Europe or the NBA. So the CBA has always been a league of who's going to survive. In fact there are CBA teams that don't bring in their good players until the end of the year. They save them, and they bring them in at the end to win the championship. That's not how I would do it, but it is the path some other teams have chosen.

We were in Great Falls for three years, and our team went to the CBA Finals twice. We won ninety games and lost forty-two during that stretch, and I was named CBA Coach of the Year twice. We never did win the league title.

SIX

TOO YOUNG TO KNOW BETTER

Players aren't the only ones in the CBA hoping to get noticed by the NBA. Three years seem like a long time when you're as far away from "The Show" as we obviously were in Great Falls. I started worrying that people in the NBA were forgetting about me.

So in 1983 I jumped at the chance to become the player personnel director for the Cleveland Cavaliers. Getting your foot in the door in the NBA at times can mean accepting a personnel position. But my ego was telling me to get back into the league.

THIS GAME'S THE BEST!

Getting into the league, even at a low position, is tougher than staying in the league, because once you're in, you develop relationships that can help you keep jobs.

I'll admit my reasons for taking the position were monetary too. Cleveland was offering a three-year contract at twice what I was earning in Montana. Money talks. The only downside was I had to wear a suit and tie every day.

The Cavs had been a really bad team for a very long time, and after watching the team practice, I wondered if I hadn't left a better team behind in Great Falls. The head coach of the Cavs was Tom Nissalke, the same guy who did not want me when the Spurs had drafted me ten years earlier. After another typically Cavalier year of twenty wins or so, management gave Nissalke the ax.

I really wanted to leave the front office and get back into coaching. So I told the owners that was something I was hoping for. To the surprise of just about everyone, they gave me the job. I was a head coach in the NBA—though Cleveland hadn't had a winning season in six years.

After getting the job in Cleveland, I'll admit I was more than a little paranoid about what people throughout the league were saying about me. At thirty-three I was the youngest coach in the NBA, and I was sure they were saying I hadn't paid my dues. My fear became a distraction.

I knew a lot of NBA people were whispering that I had played a role in Nissalke's dismissal. That happens in the league. Every time someone gets fired, if a team hires from within, someone starts a rumor about backstabbing. That accusation really hurt, because the one time I was asked my opinion of Nissalke by the club president, I said he had done a solid job. I did not feel he deserved to be fired. Nissalke's problem was that the club president, Harry Weltman, wanted him to play younger players, and he refused. The coach doesn't often win those power struggles.

But once the decision to fire Nissalke was made, I wanted to at least be considered for the position. Don Nelson, to whom I was very close at that time, told me he had called the Cavs asking for permission to interview me for an assistant's job with the Milwaukee Bucks. The Cavs wouldn't let him do it. Nellie said that Weltman gave him the impression he was going to name me coach.

Back then I really needed the job, because Cathy and I were broke. We had a house in Montana that we could not sell, and we were losing our asses. We had a house in Cleveland that cost a lot. So to make ends meet, I would take advances on my company credit card, which I'd pay back after going out on the road. There were months when I was ready to make the phone call and consider bankruptcy. It doesn't sound like a lot, but I was six or eight thousand dollars behind in debts. At the time I earned only $31,000, so that was a lot of money. Our family had expanded when Coby was born in 1983. My being on the road was the only way we could get the cash to pay all our bills.

THIS GAME'S THE BEST!

Cathy tells the story that our son, Coby, did not really know me until he was three. When I'd walk in the house, he'd run and hide behind Cathy, peeking out from behind her leg to give me a blank stare. "This is Daddy," Cathy would have to say, almost introducing me to my own son.

Well, the excitement of being one of two dozen head coaches in the NBA wore off pretty quickly. We opened the season losing nineteen of our first twenty-one games. Columnists were calling for my head, making fun of the owners who had given me this shot. We were oh and nine, then won a game in Atlanta. Then we lost ten more in a row and were two and nineteen headed into a Christmas Day game, again with Atlanta. I had really drawn the ire of my players by suggesting to the Cleveland newspaper that losing did not hurt some of them enough to reverse our fortunes. I told the paper that a couple of our players seemed to even enjoy losing. That got everyone talking.

On Christmas morning Cathy told me she wasn't going to come to the game. I was just getting killed by the fans in the Cleveland stands. There were a number of fans who would yell obscenities at me the whole game. Well, while I'm coaching, I'm so focused I do not hear them. But Cathy, who sat six rows behind the bench, heard it all. It was hard on her to hear all that ugliness directed at me. There was one kid, probably about twenty-five years old, whom she told me she was going to punch because he was so mean.

TOO YOUNG TO KNOW BETTER

Anyway, at 2–19 I told Cathy that the way things were going, if she did not come, no one would be cheering for me. I told her I had long ago accepted that fans pay their admission price, and they can say what they want—even if it is really hurtful stuff. It is part of the game. I told her that, at that stage, she was my only fan, she had to go.

Well, with Cathy in the stands, we won that game against Atlanta on Christmas, and before you knew it, we were winning every other game. Then we had several short winning streaks. We went to Chicago and beat the Bulls, then to the West Coast and beat Portland. I got thrown out of that game against Portland for, I swear, no reason at all.

That's one of the things about being a rookie coach in the NBA. In one game that year I was sitting down when a ref made a bad call. I did not even stand up, just sat there with my legs crossed and said, "That call was atrocious." He called me for a technical. I stood up and said, "That even makes that call even more atrocious." He threw me out of the game. No cuss words. The only word I used was atrocious.

But now that I'm an experienced coach I've finally earned the referees' respect. Plus, the league is letting head coaches talk more. To me that's good. I think there should be more interplay between coach and referee just as long as it is constructive. Well . . . maybe it's not exactly constructive, but just as long as it is not detrimental. I guess calling someone a dumb son of a

---

bitch all the time is probably not constructive for anyone. But I'd never do that.

As that first season rolled on, we actually became a pretty good basketball team. We got World B. Free back from injury. World—he really got upset if you called him by his given name, Lloyd—was our only bona fide scorer. We had John Bagley, Phil Hubbard, Lonnie Shelton, Roy Hinson, Mark West, Johnny Davis, Ron Anderson, and Edgar Jones. None of them was really that good, but as a team, we meshed by the end of the year.

Phil Hubbard was a leader. He wouldn't quit, he hated losing, and he just fought hard. Bagley had his best year ever. He did not have it early on, but at the end of the year he was playing as well as anybody. I made a trade-off with World. I said, "World, if you just fake the defensive end of the court and act like you're trying to do what we want you to do, I'll get you twenty shots a game." I remember sitting in the locker room saying, "But you got to fake it, you got to act like you're out there." For twenty shots a game, World would fake anything.

World was at the end of his career. He was at the stage where the only thing he could do was score points. There was no question we needed that. But I had to have a commitment from him on both ends of the court. When he did not give it to me, I started giving him fewer minutes. That had never happened to World.

TOO YOUNG TO KNOW BETTER

It worked. After the All-Star Game I believe we compiled the fourth best record in the NBA. And World faked defense.

Coming into the last game of the season at home against the New Jersey Nets, we knew that a win would get us into the playoffs—for the first time in nine years. The fans, the same ones who had almost driven my wife from the arena, gave me a standing ovation.

We won, 114–100, and the crowd stayed around for the players to come back for a second ovation. The players got so excited, they carried me off the court on their shoulders. I've never seen that in pro basketball. The player who was the first to lift me up was World B. Free. Obviously, I was a lot skinnier then!

In the playoffs, we faced the Celtics in the first round. It was a five-game series, and we had the lead in every game with two minutes to go. Unfortunately, we won only one and they won three. Our win was by seven points; theirs were by two, three, and two. Then they went on to win the NBA title.

It was a great ending. From two–nineteen to playing tough with the champions. I was given a key to the city by the mayor. Life was good.

Expectations were high for my second year. But things fell apart as quickly as they had come together a year earlier. The team was somewhat old to begin with and had really overachieved. In the second year Lonnie Shelton came back larger, but only in his waist size. Johnny Davis was a holdout. Phil Hubbard had had a career the year before, however in year two, he became just what he was: a good player. And World simply could not get it done anymore. It was time for World to become a bench player and deliver an offensive spark off the bench. He wasn't going to accept that. His ego made him say, "No way, man— I'm still a great player." I probably should have called him in and had this discussion, but I was young and immature too. Because I did not, our relationship soured. I think World was a guy who respected honesty and directness.

But my biggest problem was with the man who had hired me, team president Harry Weltman. We had two young players, Mel Turpin and Keith Lee. The same problem Harry had faced with Nissalke he was having with me. Harry decided I should be playing the young guys more. I disagreed. The problem grew to the point that he was constantly critiquing who I was playing, how I was coaching. I think it's very difficult to critique a coach or a player on a daily basis. It seemed as if every game he wanted to talk about whether I knew I had a foul to take in the third quarter, or why I did not call time-out in a certain situation. The public doesn't understand that coaches second-guess ourselves more than anyone else. A lot of the questions you ask we do not have the answers to, because we often act from an instinctive feel for the game or situation. We believe a given decision is right when we make it, but we do not always know why we make it.

TOO YOUNG TO KNOW BETTER

And even if it turns out to be wrong, I still think when a coach makes a decision, you have to allow him that, and you have to trust that he knows what he's doing. If a coach is wimpy in his decision-making, the players are going to feel it. If a coach is uncertain in the direction he wants to take his team, players feel that. And so you do not want to do anything that raises the level of uncertainty. When your club president is questioning your every move, that raises the level of uncertainty. I tried to explain that to Harry. It did not work.

During the really down days of that second year, I received a call from the University of Pittsburgh, which had an opening for head basketball coach. I consider myself a loyal person, but it seemed like something to at least look at. I asked Harry Weltman for permission to go interview for the job. I took a day-trip to Pittsburgh to talk, meeting with the university president and a number of alumni. I thought the job was mine if I wanted it. When I got back, Weltman was pissed off. He said he gave me permission to go to Pitt but not to spend the whole day. He started questioning my loyalty, which really hurt.

Still, the Cavs' owner had assured Cathy and me that things would work out and told us to start looking for a new house in Cleveland, which the team was going to help us finance. On Friday, Cathy called owner Gordon Gund's right-hand man, who was president of the stadium corporation, and told him she had

----

found the home we wanted. He set up a meeting for Monday to arrange the deal.

Then on Sunday, Harry called me at home and fired me. He fired me over the phone. Cathy picked up the phone, called Gund's partner, and asked him what was up. He said he had heard nothing about it. He called back a few minutes later and said Gund knew nothing about it either. Weltman had made the decision without consulting either of his bosses. They called Harry at home, and he said, yes, he had fired me. They told me they were furious but that in the Cavs' corporate structure, Harry had the power to do that.

I was not surprised that they fired Harry a month to the day after he had fired me. They actually fired Harry and used me as a consultant on who to hire as Harry's replacement and also who to hire as coach. I recommended Wayne Embry, whom they hired and who is still there, working in the front office.

One of the reasons Harry gave when he fired me was what he called a lack of loyalty, which he said I showed by looking at the Pitt job *that he had given me permission to interview for!* It really upset me. What Harry did not know was that during this whole time, Don Nelson of the Milwaukee Bucks was calling, trying to get me to talk to the new owners of the Golden State Warriors, who were friends of his.

So Harry was telling everybody I was going to Pittsburgh. No one knew about Golden State. No one knew about the card I had

----

in my back pocket. But because of Harry's comments, everyone around the league heard I was disloyal.

It's funny, but when Harry fired me in mid-season, Nellie called to offer congratulations. He figured that by getting fired with twenty games to go in the season and a difficult schedule, I had probably saved myself fifteen losses off my lifetime record. That's how bad we were in year two.

I made mistakes in Cleveland, do not get me wrong. My ego was big, and I'm sure I was difficult to deal with. I just wish I had been there long enough to correct those mistakes. The way it ended was far too bitter.

The one thing I regret about my time in Cleveland is that Harry Weltman gave me my opportunity both to get back into the league and then to be a head coach at age thirty-three. Yet he and I do not talk to each other because he also fired me a year and a half later. I'm sorry that I do not communicate with the man who gave me my big break. But as I look back on it, I do not know why it had to turn out that way. I do not know if I was out of control. Management thought I was. I thought I was manageable, but maybe they did not. I think it's a lot like my coaching Shawn Kemp and Gary Payton. They have a lot of talent, just as I did. But they also have some craziness to them. It would have been easier to trade Shawn and Gary, to get tamer, older professionals. In managing in the NBA you have to accept the challenge of handling youth and passion.

THIS GAME'S THE BEST!

I think Harry gave up on me because I was too emotional, too stubborn, too opinionated. Instead of managing or maybe correcting that, he opted to look for someone he could control. I'm glad we never gave up on Gary Payton and Shawn Kemp, because they are competitors. I wish Harry hadn't given up on me, because I would have been equally as competitive for him. I wish he had worked to make me a better coach.

Cleveland was water under the bridge. So I reached for the card I hadn't played earlier and called Nellie about help with Golden State.

First, though, I went to work with Nellie and the Bucks in the playoffs. He had asked me to come up and scout opponents for him. Fortunately, that was the year they went to the finals of the conference, beating Philadelphia in the second round. The Bucks had a good team, and by being involved, I was around basketball.

As soon as the playoffs were over, I flew to San Francisco to talk with the new owners of the Warriors. The Golden State coach at the time was Johnny Bach, but the owners let him go as soon as the season ended. I was nervous about getting the Warriors job because, while Nellie told me I was in, the owners kept interviewing a couple of other guys. I had already decided that if it did not work out, I'd go looking for a college job, or maybe Nellie would have a spot on his staff. It is always nice to know there are some "life vests" out there—people you know will help you—when you've got no boat to float on. For me, Nellie was a life vest. Coach Smith was another.

The basketball business is so strange. Good coaches often do not get hired. Average coaches get new jobs. The reasons behind why a guy gets hired in this league are constantly changing. Sometimes it's because he's young, sometimes because he's old. Sometimes because he can relate to players, sometimes because he's a disciplinarian. I'm not saying that's right or wrong, or good or bad, but there's no question the rules of what kind of guy is in vogue are always changing. That makes being unemployed particularly nerve-racking.

Finally, I was offered the Warriors job and jumped at the chance. It was a lot like Cleveland when I got there. The team had been mediocre and had gone ten years without making the playoffs. But the owners seemed great. The city was fantastic. The team was becoming more talented. Plus, management wanted an up-tempo game, which I really wanted to run. And they had the players to do it.

It was an interesting team from my standpoint, because it had a center: Joe Barry Carroll. And even though Joe and I had our problems, having a guy to throw the ball to is always a luxury in this game. They had some good young players in Chris Mullin and Sleepy Floyd. Purvis Short was solid all around. Larry Smith was a very tough player and rebounder. The bench was okay, with Terry Teagle and Jerome Whitehead.

THIS GAME'S THE BEST!

The first year, everything really gelled. We won forty-four games and shocked everyone by making the playoffs. We upset Utah in the first round in one of the best comebacks of all time. They had us down two-nothing in a five-game series, and we were the first team in three decades to come back and win three straight.

To show you how far the NBA has come, the deciding fifth game in Utah took place on a Sunday, and it wasn't sold out. That wasn't but ten years ago. Imagine a fifth game in Utah not being sold out today.

We played the Lakers in the second round with Kareem Abdul-Jabbar, Magic Johnson, and James Worthy. I became the news for a few days when my temper got the best of me. Joe Barry Carroll was just driving me nuts. He had so much talent, but little heart.

We played a Saturday-Sunday back-to-back in Oakland. On Saturday we were awful. We got beaten very easily. After the game I was yelling at the team in the locker room, and Joe Barry basically said, "Coach, why don't you just relax? We're not good enough to beat the Lakers. We've had a great year, why don't you just relax and cool down."

He was giving up. He was saying we weren't good enough to beat the Lakers—which was, by the way, the truth. But you do not admit that truth in the middle of battle.

I was stunned. I went and did the postgame press conference, and by the time I got back to the locker room, I was boiling. I just went crazy on Joe Barry's locker. I threw a ball at it. I ripped the door off its hinges. I started throwing his stuff all over the locker room. When I was done, I just looked at one of our trainers and asked him to get it fixed before our game the next day.

The funny part is that Joe Barry had showered and was long gone by the time I went nuts. When he showed up the next day, everything was back in order. The value of my tirade was completely lost on him. The whole mess would have been nothing if a reporter hadn't walked into the locker room five minutes after I was done and asked people what had happened. It became a pretty big story in the local media.

In the end, Joe Barry was right. We could not play with the Lakers, and they won the series. We lost a seven-game series in five games. We beat the Lakers in Game Four, when Sleepy Floyd scored fifty-one points in a great game. But we lost Game Five down in L.A.

I do not know if Joe Barry even talked to me until the following fall. The next meeting I had with him was in my office in September. We talked for about an hour and a half. We talked about intensity and what I expected. I asked him if he could play for me. He said he could. It was all bullshit. He's a big philosopher. He's one of those books you read and you think every day, as you're reading it, that there's a different ending, a different meaning to it.

In my opinion Joe Barry was a very talented player who just

did not want to make a commitment to be a consistent player. A worker. He was happy with being a good player half the time and being a lazy player half the time. I told management that. I do not believe your star can have that personality. He'll kill you. Joe Barry would walk into a practice and if he was seven minutes early, he would sit down and read the newspaper or a book in the stands as everybody else was loosening up, until one minute before practice. If you'd say something, he'd respond with, "I'm here on time."

And he would read books in the locker room before a game. I'm all for education and expanding your horizons, but that just drove me batty. We'd have guys like Mullin and Larry Smith, guys who are fierce about their game preparation. Chris was always nervous before a game. Larry Smith was ready to tear someone up. Then over in the corner would be Joe Barry, his legs crossed, reading *The Wall Street Journal.*

The team changed a lot before that second season. Mullin went into alcohol rehab. We traded for Ralph Sampson, then he got hurt. Larry Smith got hurt. We traded Purvis Short because we wanted to give Terry Teagle the sixth-man job. Then Teagle pulled a hamstring and was out a big part of the year. Joe Barry didn't come to camp in shape. He had a "Screw you" mentality toward me. And we had the Chris Washburn problem that year too. A talented center who had been a star in college, Chris was suspended and sent to rehab, so we had him distracting the team all the time with episodes of drugs, lateness, craziness, stupid stuff.

We were starting a lineup that had only a slight resemblance to the lineup we had planned on. At one stage our starting point guard was a guy we had cut because he wasn't even the fifth-best guard in our camp. We brought him in one day, and he started the next game. All of a sudden you are playing with your eighth, ninth, and tenth men on a really bad team.

But the guys worked hard and I think got better, so that made losing a little more tolerable. I had a team that gave me everything they could give me, and we could not win. I mean, we would have the lead going in to the five-minute mark of the fourth quarter, and we did not have any answers down the stretch, just did not have the talent.

I was coaching hard. In fact, I honestly think that season might have been one of my best coaching jobs ever, and we were sixteen and forty-eight. We were awful.

To make matters even more interesting, I suddenly had a new boss. It should have been the greatest thing in the world to have Don Nelson, my mentor, as the new general manager of the Warriors. Instead, it was a nightmare. Not a day went by when someone wasn't mentioning that one of the best coaches in NBA history was sitting right there in the general manager's office and that if things did not work out with me . . . People were pulling me aside and warning me to watch my back. But I always argued that he was my friend and had helped me get the job. Still, his presence made every loss just a little more worrisome. For the first time, I believed I was in an organization where I could not find my support. Nellie kept saying he was not going to take over for me, but everyone else had a different opinion.

Toward the end of that year I had a feeling things weren't going to last. So I asked Nellie to go on a walk with me. We took a stroll in the parking lot, and again I asked him about the rumors that he was going to take over. I said, "Every city I go into they say you're going to take over for me. Every town— everything is you and me. Nobody mentions that our players are working so hard, playing above their heads. Can't you change that?" I told him that all management had to do was give me a contract extension and then everyone's focus would be on the floor. I said it doesn't even have to be guaranteed, just make some type of statement so that everybody can get off of the subject of Nellie and George. I was asking him to change the atmosphere. I was not asking for more commitment or money.

When Nellie told me he could not promise that, I knew I was done. I was fired, and to the surprise of almost no one, the next coach was . . . Don Nelson.

I honestly do not think that Nellie wanted to take the job from me, but when I say that, people in the NBA ask me how I can be so naive. I personally do not think he wanted to coach that team, but because of his financial situation—he was going through a divorce at the time—I think it made sense for him. That's my perception of the circumstances.

Within days I started getting calls with rumors from around the country. One was that I had demanded a long-term contract or threatened to walk. The other was that I was in alcohol rehab. Now I'm a happy partyer, but I do not drink very often to the point of inebriation. Yet suddenly these crazy accusations were coming out.

Years later the rehab rumor was one that stuck to me. When the Sonics called about their job in 1991, General Manager Bob Whitsitt said any contract had to include a clause that kept me from alcohol during the season. Unfortunately, that clause has gotten a lot of attention. I had no problem signing it. Whitsitt wanted a comfort zone, and I had no problem giving him that. I think he did it to help me control myself in a way. I think it was very smart. It's actually worked out better than I thought it would. I do feel better because I do not drink during the year, and I have no problem living without alcohol.

A number of people have tried to lump the Cleveland and Golden State situations together in a pattern. Overachieves the first year. Falls out with superstars. Bottoms out in second year. Implodes while arguing with management. I just can't buy it. Those kinds of cookie-cutter explanations ignore too many of the other factors involved in each situation.

One thing is for sure: I learned an awful lot from both expe-

----

riences, and I probably wouldn't be where I am today without them—even the bad stuff.

After being fired for the second time in two years, I pretty much just buried myself in the house. I did not speak to Nellie for months. I was unemployed again. But this time I felt as if I did not have any "life vests" to hold onto.

SEVEN

MY OWN PURGATORY

A lot of people thought I'd run from basketball after the ugly ending with Golden State in 1988. And if I did not run, they figured I'd at least hide out as an assistant coach somewhere, tucked away in obscurity.

I did neither. Instead, I ran to my own version of purgatory— back to the CBA—and took a head-coaching job. I think my reaction was seen for what it was: a way of showing the world I could still coach. And I could still win! My choice for revenge was to keep winning games. And I think deep down inside I like that choice now more than ever. It was one of the best decisions I ever made, because I did not have to kiss anyone's butt to get back into the league. I was able to do it the hard way.

Almost no coach who has been cut loose in the NBA has ever made a similar move.

After being fired from Golden State I had the good fortune to have the Warriors committed to paying my salary for the next year, whether or not I worked. That gave me a lot of flexibility in deciding what to do next.

Cathy and I were having a hard time living in the city where I'd been fired. So we decided we needed a house somewhere that we could always call home, a place we could always go back to, no matter what. That's why we decided to buy a house in Idaho. I knew I'd never get fired in Idaho. You can't. Idaho doesn't even know about the NBA, let alone have a team. I've gone to the bars in Idaho and asked if they could put on an NBA game. They told me no, because studio wrestling was on and they did not like the NBA. I kind of liked that.

One of the commitments I had made before leaving Golden State was to serve as a commentator during the annual CBA draft. Jim Drucker, who used to be the commissioner of the CBA, had decided to broadcast the draft on television. He asked me to come analyze the draft with the NBA's Marty Blake.

While we were off the air, Gary Holle of the Albany Patroons mentioned that he was searching for a coach. He asked me for a list of possible candidates. Vanity aside, I suggested myself. He asked if I would really be interested. I said sure, but at some obnoxious figure for CBA coaching. I think I asked for a hundred thousand. We basically laughed and left it at that.

It was August, and nothing was on the horizon. I was antsy—I wanted to coach . . . bad. When September rolls around I usually like getting to the gym, but I was hanging out on the golf course and on the beach and driving people crazy. I was hanging out with my former Spur teammate Coby Dietrick, who lived in Ventura, California.

Anyway, I mentioned my conversation with Holle to Cathy, telling her that I basically turned down a job to coach in the CBA. She said, "Why'd you do that?" I told her I did not think she'd want to move to Albany, New York. Since neither of us knew anything about Albany, we got out the atlas and looked. I had heard it was beautiful there. After reading a little about Albany—and thinking how miserable it would be to live a year with me unemployed—Cathy encouraged me to call Albany.

I like the CBA, and I liked the idea of going back to the East Coast, near where I had grown up. The job was for just five months. In the CBA you start in mid-October and are done by mid-March, unless you make the playoffs, which add another month. So if you're a guy looking for another job, one great thing about the CBA is you finish early enough in the year so you can still catch on with an NBA team that needs scouting help while looking to make a late-season playoff run.

I have to admit I went to Albany that year moaning, groaning, and complaining. I wanted to coach, but I still wasn't over not being in the NBA. The first year with the Patroons I tried to attend many of the postgame parties for the fans. One bar always hosted our team after games and gave us free drinks. The bar owner would complain because we had a guy on our team named Greg Grissom, who's about six-eleven, two eighty. He could drink a lot of beer. Between Greg and I, we could drink thirty-five beers in a night. I don't think he made any profit off of our postgame parties!

The town was really good to me. The fans treated me well. It seemed everyone knew I was a coach with NBA experience who had come there to rebuild their team in a city that had won the CBA championship in numerous years with Phil Jackson and Bill Musselman. Albany had a tradition of winning. I kind of fit in in Albany—a blue-collar guy in a blue-collar town. I was just hanging out. I wasn't very animated. I was just George.

I became more popular when, during a game against Wichita Falls, I jumped in for one of my players who was being harassed by the opposing coach. I shoved the coach, almost fought him during a playoff game. He touched one of my players, and I pushed him and shouted, "Do not ever touch one of my players!" The fans loved that. I guess everyone wants a boss who will fight for them.

One thing—the rowdy crowds—hadn't changed since I last coached in the CBA. One night in Wichita Falls the owners gave away miniature basketballs to the first two thousand fans. When we started winning, the crowd used the balls to pelt the referees, then they threw them at us. It got so crazy, we had to leave the floor with time on the clock.

My strength in Albany came from a guy by the name of Gerald Oliver. Gerald is a wonderful basketball man and a wonderful human being. He was our player personnel director and assistant coach. If it wasn't for Gerald and his knowledge of the league, and his friendship that year, I could've self-destructed.

Gerald pumped me up, did not let me pout. He constantly told me I not only deserved to be in the NBA, I was one of the top-ten coaches in the world. Gerald was the first guy who ever told me that. I'm not sure I could ever believe that, but I was having an especially tough time in Albany. Gerald has been with a lot of good coaches. He's been in basketball a long, long, long time.

He would bitch at me in a very friendly way about doing the right things. He advised me not to take the NBA scouts and personnel guys out for drinks, especially after the Golden State accusations. He said I should not let the NBA folks who visited us

THIS GAME'S THE BEST!

there see me drinking at all due to the perception. He helped me deal with my referee issues and my temper. He was a smart man and a good friend to help me steer around potential problems.

I learned a lot from Gerald. He was right in encouraging me to show some discipline. As the season progressed, I tried to do that.

Although our team was good it was not memorable that season. We topped the division, won thirty-eight games and lost eighteen. We did not start a guy whose name anyone would remember, but our players were probably the best executing offensive team I've ever had—executing basic plays, trick plays, and cute stuff all the time.

We lost in the semifinals of the playoffs to Wichita Falls, the team whose coach I had challenged to a fight. All in all, not a bad year, and a great learning experience.

After the year in Albany, I was offered the chance to go to Spain and coach one of the most famous of all basketball teams: Real Madrid. The job came up suddenly. Once the season was over, I was hoping to maybe get an NBA job, but this was an opportunity I could not miss.

I love tradition, and Real Madrid has more tradition in the sport than maybe any team in the world. If you were to go around the world and ask people about the Boston Celtics or Real Madrid, I bet you more people would know Real Madrid. Now most people are familiar with Real Madrid because of its soccer team,

MY OWN PURGATORY

but it also is the only team in Europe that's won eight European championships in basketball. The next highest number is probably three. Real Madrid's trophy room is so spectacular I actually invited friends and others over just to see the collection of silver and gold cups and statues that fills a room half the size of a basketball court. Artists should go there just to admire the sculptures on some of those trophies. It puts the Boston Celtics trophy room completely to shame.

Real Madrid is a club, a basketball club, which has players starting at age twelve. There is a twelve-year-old team, a fourteen-year-old team, a sixteen-year-old team, an eighteen-year-old team, and then there is the professional team. There are other clubs throughout Europe that the teams compete against. Real Madrid is a soccer and basketball club—it does both. The truth is, it's a soccer club that supports basketball. When I was there, Real Madrid had ten soccer players making a million dollars a year. And it had a soccer stadium that seated a hundred and twenty thousand people.

But the basketball team had its own very successful tradition. The reason they hired me was because Real Madrid had won twenty-five of the last twenty-nine Spanish championships. But they had lost the last three years to their arch-rival Barcelona. They wanted a change; they wanted to continue the winning tradition. And they thought an American guy who had coached in the NBA had the chance to continue that tradition.

THIS GAME'S THE BEST!

I really enjoyed my time and the people I met in Spain. There were crazy experiences and situations, but they were filled with passionate, good people I will never forget.

Clearly, one of the most emotional periods of my life was the three days following the death of our star player Fernando Martin. His death will be as vivid a memory to me as anything I have ever gone through.

Fernando died in a car accident on his way to a game on a Sunday. But when we showed up at the arena and learned of Fernando's accident, we canceled the game. It felt like a national day of mourning. Fernando was the Spanish basketball equivalent of Michael Jordan, in terms of his popularity within the country. As a person, he was one of the most powerful people I've ever been around.

He was a big man, about six-eight, two fifty. Shoulders wide, waist thin. Women thought he was gorgeous. He always wore a little beard. Dark eyes, black hair, a really attractive man. We'd walk into a room, and everybody would pay attention to Fernando. He had movie-star looks and the reverence of Julius Erving.

His power was in his eyes and the way he carried himself, his demeanor. He appeared fearless. For all that, he was not a great basketball player. But he was a great winner. He loved doing the dirty work. He had played in the NBA for a year in Portland. He was the best player in Spain and Portland brought him over, but it did not work out, and he missed Spain so he went back.

Well, on Monday morning after the accident his coffin was laid out in our stadium. The stadium, called the City of Sport, seats probably eight thousand. We as a team were the first people to view his body. It wasn't pretty because the accident was brutal. It was the first time I met Fernando's mother, who sat there and spoke Spanish to me for quite a while. I guess she did not know that I did not understand Spanish. Fernando's brother, Antonio, was interpreting, telling me that Fernando loved me and thought I was the most exciting coach he'd ever played for. Antonio also was on our team. It was just an incredibly emotional moment. She looked at me and said, "My son is your son."

That night they opened the stadium for the viewing of the body. The mass was around eight o'clock. It took forty-five minutes for the service. The building was packed. After the mass, the crowd stood and gave Fernando a forty-five–minute standing ovation. They stood there and clapped for forty-five minutes straight. It gave me goose bumps.

Then came the public viewing. People filed by the casket until six o'clock in the morning. I was told by the players that Fernando was compared to a James Dean–type figure. He was a rebel in real life, and when he died everybody related to him and respected him.

THIS GAME'S THE BEST!

There were twenty buses of people headed to the cemetery for his funeral, including the Real Madrid soccer team, the Spanish football association, the basketball association, and three or four teams that brought their players and clubs to honor Fernando. The day began with a little religious ceremony in which his body was christened, and then the body had to be taken out to the hearse. But no one had arranged to carry out the casket. And so it was carried out of the building on the shoulders of our players, and it was weird, because they carried it up above their heads, as if they were lifting him up to a higher being.

The buses made about a ten-mile procession to the cemetery. The entire route was lined with people waving, screaming, holding signs. When we got to the cemetery, the entrance had an arch that the buses could not get through. By the time twenty busloads of people had walked from the entrance to the grave site, the casket was already in the ground. I said to Cathy that Fernando was just sitting up there in heaven laughing at all of us wandering through the mud in this huge cemetery looking for his grave site. It was the only thing that was funny about that day.

I told the team to meet after the ceremony at the hotel. I remember sitting with Chechu Biriukov, who was one of Fernando's good friends, and Quique Villalobos and Jose Llorente, who both spoke very good English. The four of us just sat there. They were all crying and telling stories, and Chechu was cussing out Fernando, saying, "Stubborn SOB . . . you shouldn't have been driving so fast." The police said Fernando was going over a hundred miles an hour when he wrecked; his car flipped seven times.

We had a game that night, and I said to the team, "If you do not want to play, you do not have to play." The players said, "If we did not play, Fernando would think we were a bunch of pussies. We've got to play."

For all the bravado, no one felt like playing. We had no preparation because we had been at the funeral.

So here we were getting ready to play a European Cup game, and two hours before the game, we're all crying and wiped out. So we all went up and took a quick nap before going to the game. We were losing by twenty-two points at halftime, just getting whipped. As you might suspect, we had no energy; we weren't even running. We did not know if Antonio was going to play, but when he showed we had to play him. He was horrible. He had no business playing that night, but he felt as if he had to because his brother would've wanted him to.

I went into the locker room, and because I knew so little Spanish I did not say much. On the way out one of the players said, "Let's do it for Fernando."

We won the game by twenty-two. We had a forty-four–point turnaround in the second half. I mean, it was over quick too. We made up the twenty-two points we were behind in the first

THIS GAME'S THE BEST!

---

five minutes of the second half. We went up by two a minute later, and the rout was on. Unbelievable. It was the biggest comeback I've ever been associated with.

But the win wasn't the most eerie part. That came before the game. The players put Fernando's jersey on the bench, draping it over a chair. They put his shorts on the seat of the chair and his shoes underneath it. Before the game the opposing team ran down and threw roses at the feet of this empty chair. I was stunned. And I had to coach the entire game with his empty chair there.

We went into the locker room after the game, and Antonio was bawling, Chechu was bawling, everybody was bawling. In Europe, if the crowd wants the team to come back, they chant. Almost like a rock concert. The crowd that night was chanting as loud as I'd ever heard them. What the fans were chanting was *"Fernando esta aquí,"* which means "Fernando is here, Fernando is here."

They wouldn't stop chanting *"Fernando esta aquí, Fernando esta aquí."* Fernando's mother was in the president's box, crying, waving, and throwing kisses to the crowd. I was just shaking my head. I was so taken by the power of the moment that I didn't leave the court. The players walked off the court a second time, but the crowd kept chanting, *"Fernando esta aquí!"*

Then the players all came running back onto the court again, only this time they ran up the aisle to the president's box to give a hug to Fernando's mother. Wow!

MY OWN PURGATORY

It was powerful.

Unfortunately, that was the high point and the low point of our season. After that, Antonio had an emotionally tough time—he lost thirty pounds, and we had to give him a couple of weeks off. Chechu, our next-best Spanish player, tore a knee up, had knee surgery, and was out the year. Quique, who was kind of our bench guy, broke his foot. He would play on weekends and get through the pain with the help of medical treatments, but he never practiced. And in Europe you can't pick players up. If you lose three players in the club system, you have to play your younger players. Well, we never got to the point where we had to play a younger player, but we had a kid on our team that plays at Wake Forest now, Ricky Peral. He was on our team at sixteen, and he was starting to play because we had only seven guys that could suit up.

After the season, the club president decided he did not want me back, so he told reporters I was a jinx. The rumor on the street was that they had already fired me but just hadn't told me. But I found out they had already hired the guy for next year, an American named Wayne Brabender. I knew the rumor was true when I went to a writer and said, and this is a quote, "You can write this: 'If they hire Wayne Brabender, it will be the biggest mistake Real Madrid basketball will ever make.' I said I want that in the paper tomorrow, the big sports paper, *Marca*." He did not write it. He came back the next day and said his editor wouldn't let him write it. The editor knew Brabender had already been hired.

One of the club president's criticisms, oddly enough, was that I "coached like an American." Spanish basketball, by and large, has been a game that stressed walking the ball up the court. All European basketball is now being influenced by the Yugoslavians, who play slowly. To them, scoring in the sixties is a good game. I'm trying to score ninety. Our team scored 110 points, and I was being criticized. The press said I was not adapting to Spanish basketball. I was confused.

It has taken me a few years to figure out what a mistake I made by taking on the press. There are easier ways to go through life. There are ways to work with the press. I just never tried them. I think it's my rebellious nature. I do not know if it's fighting authority or fighting power, but it has not been until the last couple of years that I've begun to figure this out. I am still learning.

The summer following our season, I had no clue what I was going to do next. I was offered a job in Greece, but Cathy said she did not want to take the kids there while the Gulf War situation was so hot. She was going to go back, and I was going to take the job when I decided instead to go for one more shot at the CBA.

So when the opportunity came once again to return to Albany

as head coach, I did not hesitate. But when we made the decision to come back, we did it with a goal in mind: to make the season something exceptional, something memorable.

We did that . . . in a huge way. We set out to break a record. The best record ever posted by a professional basketball team was 48–6. No one thought anyone could break that record. We broke it. We went 50–6. My staff said from the very beginning that our team was special, and the players lived up to that expectation. That team had a confidence and an attitude that was tough as nails.

We were so good that the CBA All-Star Team of ten had three players from our team: Vincent Askew, Mario Elie, and Clinton Smith. During the game I had a run-in with Anthony Mason, now with the Charlotte Hornets. He had turned the ball over a couple of times, and I called a time-out and said, "Just relax, guy. We've got the lead, just take your time, be responsible, let's make sure we run some time off the clock, get a shot, just simple stuff." He thought I was picking on him, so he went off on me in front of the other guys. I said, "You sit your ass down and shut up." I took him out, and we won the game.

The next week our Albany team played Tulsa, where Mason was averaging thirty points a game. My players who had been at the All-Star Game told the rest of our team about Anthony's attempt to show me up. Our guys took it personally. They decided on their own to shut Anthony Mason down. He never scored a field goal. Ben McDonald was a great defender. He just took Mason on as his own project.

Mason actually did us a favor because we were so good that year we needed things like that to motivate us. We always liked playing against teams or players who were on some kind of roll. We loved the teams that came in and had won ten in a row. That happened a couple of times, and we beat those teams by at least forty points.

We did not play any chicken games that year, though it might not have been a bad idea. We played in a brand-new building that seated about fifteen thousand people. I do not know if we ever had a crowd over three thousand. During that second year in Albany, I think the fans became bored with us. When you win your home games by an average of twenty points, there is not a lot of suspense or excitement in the games.

That team provided me with as much fun as any I've ever been around. We lost in the Western Conference, but we sent four guys to the NBA and three guys to Europe before the playoffs ended, so we were down to nothing, basically. It would have been great to win a title with those guys that year, but when players had the chance to make more money in the NBA or Europe, I could not tell them not to go. Even if we were in the playoffs.

Actually, I almost wasn't there to enjoy all that success. We had started that season something like 10–0 and were taking the team over to a fan's house for Thanksgiving dinner. On the way out the door, the phone rang. It was a basketball friend who said he had another job for me, in Zaragoza, Spain. He said the team really wanted me and was willing to pay me almost five times what I was earning in Albany.

The catch was that Zaragoza wanted me right away. I said, "I can't go now—the season is just starting." He told me to go to dinner and think it over, then call him back later. He was sure the money angle would change my mind.

On the drive over to dinner, Cathy and I talked it over, and I think we were both changing our minds, that maybe we did need to take this job in Zaragoza. We figured we would get Terry Stotts, who by then had become our assistant coach, to take over the team and it would be a good deal for everyone.

Well, while we were sitting at dinner somebody started asking each player why he was there and what he was thankful for. The first player, Vincent Askew, said, "Because of George." So our host Pat Riley, a local businessman (not the coach), said, "Are all of you here because of George?" Everyone said yeah, and started telling stories about where they could have gone. But they came to Albany, most said, because they believed I was the coach who could get them into the NBA.

Both Cathy and I were shocked. She asked the players what would happen if I left. Ben McDonald said, "Let me put it this way—if I was in the middle of one-and-one and had shot one free

THIS GAME'S THE BEST!

----

throw and somebody came up and whispered in my ear that George was leaving, I'd walk off the court right in the middle of the game and go with him."

I said, "You're kidding me. If they bring somebody else in you'd still have a shot at the NBA." As a group they shook their head no.

On the drive home that night, Cathy and I said, almost in unison, that there was no way we could leave that team. Can you imagine the headlines: "Coach jumps ship, abandons the team and six players go with him!" And the players who were most vocal were our stars Vincent Askew, Ben McDonald, and Mario Elie.

When we got home I called my friend and told him no thanks. He called me every name in the book. He was so sure I was going that he'd already made reservations for us. We did not speak to each other for almost two years because of my decision.

That spring the president of the Real Madrid club was up for re-election. In Europe the members of the club elect the president, who makes most of the business decisions. The guy who ran against the incumbent president had declared, "If I win, I'll bring back George Karl."

That turned out to be such a popular idea among the club voters that suddenly both candidates were in favor of it. Imagine: George Karl as a campaign issue!

So it did not matter who won, because both of them had prom-

----

ised that Cathy and I were going back to Spain for the next season. All this was going on while my Albany team was beating teams left and right, and it was funny that no one in the CBA ever mentioned a word. It did not become a distraction at all.

While we were rocking and rolling in Albany, Real Madrid had already fired Wayne Brabender in mid-season, and the team was going through all types of hell. Real Madrid hired an older coach, and he had a heart attack during one of the European Cup Games—collapsed on the court in the middle of a game. He would die some five months later. The team was in tremendous disarray.

The guy who won the election as president of the Real Madrid club came to the United States that spring to offer me a deal. Our season in Albany was over at the time, and I had taken a short-term job scouting for Golden State in the playoffs. Don Nelson had called and offered me the chance to show people in the NBA that I was still around.

Even though I was working with Golden State, I thought my best deal the next year was going to come in Spain. When the new president of Real Madrid showed up, I knew I was right. I received an unbelievable offer.

We came back and won a lot of games. But I became frustrated when the press, with whom I had already lost favor, accused me of throwing a game against Forum Valladolid. Arvidas Sabonis, who is now with the Portland Trail Blazers, was on that Zaragosa team, and we got beat so badly that the press accused me of throwing the game. The truth is, it was one of those games in which it did not matter what I did—I could not get the team going. In sports, we all have those nights.

I was still having a hard time dealing with the criticism that my coaching was "too American." In Spain the philosophy is to play only six players. Sometimes coaches play only their starting five the whole game. Well, I played many more players, rotated them in and out, and people just could not deal with it. They wondered what I was doing.

My Spanish was better but still not great during my second tour. The kids, though, were in school there, so they were learning the language well. One time we were driving home from a game, and I asked Kelci to get out the Spanish dictionary and look up the word *mierda.* I thought it was a derivative of the word *mira,* which I knew meant "look here." The players had been yelling *mierda* at me all night, so I wanted to know what it meant. "Dad," Kelci said, "it means 'shit.' "

The language barrier was always an issue for me. When I got the job the first time, Cathy asked me how much Spanish I had learned. I told her none, which was true. Once I was there, I took Spanish classes every day. But by the time I left the second go-around, I spoke well enough to do interviews.

I had two American players on that team, but neither one knew Spanish. My lifesaver was an assistant coach that had been in the

MY OWN PURGATORY

Spanish league for twenty-eight years. His name was Clifford Luyk. An American who had played for Real Madrid when he was younger, he was now married to a Spanish woman and had given up his U.S. citizenship.

Clifford translated for me. As well as two of the players, Jose Llorente and Quique Villalobos. It was funny when the players told me a couple of times that Clifford wasn't translating exactly what I had said. Sometimes he was translating it into what he thought they should do. But Clifford was a godsend for me, although his translations with the media did not always square with my own words!

Only a couple of the players I had coached two years earlier were still around. Still, the team would go on to win the Rey Copa Cup that year, which is like the silver medal of European basketball.

So in four years I had coached in Albany, gone home to Idaho, coached in Madrid, gone home to Idaho, gone back to Albany, gone home to Idaho, then gone back to Madrid. And my family went with me every move. In fact, my kids never finished classes in the school they started in during those four years.

But through it all, I never entertained the thought of getting out of coaching altogether. I just liked it too much. I liked the competition . . . in any language.

EIGHT

THE
RESCUE

On New Year's Eve, 1991, during my last season in Spain, Cathy and I went out for dinner at a Chinese restaurant in Madrid. The waiter said we had to eat twelve grapes at midnight for good luck—which was exactly what we were hoping for in the next year.

Over dinner we decided it was about time to give up hope that anyone in the NBA was going to hire me again. We decided that in that next year I would look for a good college job. We thought that with Coach Smith in my corner and my record in the CBA and Europe that I could probably get a college graduate assistant's job. Then in a couple of years I could get at least a head job at some small school and work my way up that way.

The next night we had dinner with some American friends who had adopted the Spanish tradition of wrapping a coin in foil and baking it in a loaf of bread. Whoever bites into the bread and gets the coin has good luck. Well, Cathy got it that year, and she boldly said, "This is going to be our year."

Little did we know.

Three weeks later Cathy was at home when Bob Whitsitt, general manager of the Seattle SuperSonics, called, looking for me. Cathy did not think much of the call, because NBA guys phoned every once in a while asking about players who were on our team or who we were playing in Europe. He politely asked Cathy how she liked Spain, and she told him how great it was. We would find out later that that was the perfect answer because it did not make us sound too eager.

Well, when I returned Bob's call, he asked if I wanted back in the league. I tried to act cool about it, but I was bursting inside. I walked out and told Cathy the Sonics were considering me for an assistant coaching job. Neither one of us could believe it.

At the time the Sonics were coached by K. C. Jones. Whitsitt said he felt that the Sonics needed more of an upbeat tempo, more energy. Bob asked if I thought I could provide that as an assistant. To take the job as K.C.'s assistant, I would have had to take a

Once a clotheshorse, always a clotheshorse. That's me at age seventeen in Penn Hills, Pennsylvania, in my senior year of high school.

In 1975, I was a San Antonio Spur in the American Basketball Association, and I loved it. I averaged 8.1 points per game, and was among the league leaders in fights.

All photos courtesy of George and Cathy Karl except where noted.

The Spurs were part of the NBA in 1977, and I'm going to the hoop against the New Orleans Jazz..

The ultimate goal of any professional athlete— getting your face on a trading card. This is my 1975 card with the Spurs. *(Photo courtesy of The Topps Company)*

Cathy and I visited Acapulco in the summer of 1975. I made those puka shells!

My first head coaching job—I became coach of the CBA Montana Golden Nuggets in Great Falls in September of 1980.

At home in Cleveland, in November of 1985 with Cathy and the kids, Kelci and Coby. Kelci is six and a half years old here; Coby's two and a half.

It's 1989, and this is a postcard of my Real Madrid team in Europe. Fernando Martin is number 10, third from the left in the back row.

Back in the NBA, in one of my first games as the coach of the Seattle Supersonics in January of 1992.

Everybody who has played for me in Seattle has been a stand-up guy. Family friend Pat Riley and I are hanging out with cutouts of Ricky Pierce, Shawn Kemp, and Derrick McKey, at the Jammin' camp in 1992.

My sister Peggy, my dad Joe, and I chow down on Easter Sunday, 1993.

To be a winner, you've got to use every edge you're given. Kelci's probably not going to take this hand. *(Photo courtesy of Seattle Times/Rod Mar)*

Everybody's smiling, including me, at this Sonics game in 1993. We must be winning by thirty points.

Relaxing in the hot tub in Burgdorf, Idaho, a town of which we are part owners. It's an old mining town with no electricity or running water. *(Photo courtesy of Seattle Times/Rod Mar)*

The home team in 1994. Clockwise from left, Cathy, Coby, Kelci, and me holding our dog Buddy. *(Photo courtesy of John McDonough/Sports Illustrated)*

That's Charles Barkley with Coby during the David Robinson Invitational in San Antonio in 1994. Charles has been tough on the Sonics, but he has been a good friend to my family.

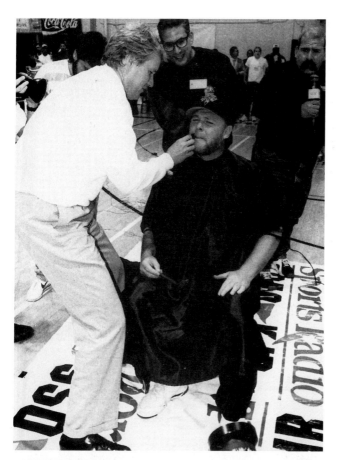

I'm getting my beard shaved before an exhibition game as part of a fund-raiser in 1994. My barber, Brent, is supervising.

If I can coach in the NBA, I can certainly lead an orchestra. I'm taking my bows after conducting the Seattle Symphony for the opening of Key Arena in 1995.
(Reprinted with permission of Seattle Post Intelligencer)

Talking to the team before a preseason game against the Lakers in Boise, Idaho, in October 1996. We bought 110 tickets for friends and family to see this game.

Just another day at the office! This temper tantrum cost me $8500, but it would have cost a lot more if Terry Stotts hadn't done such a good job of holding me back. *(Photo courtesy of Seattle Times/Rod Mar)*

Nordstrom's dresses me more tastefully than this today. Terry Stotts, me, Bobby Weiss, and Dwayne Casey at Retro Night during the NBA at 50 celebration, January 15, 1997. *(Photo courtesy of Barry Gossage)*

huge cut in pay. But the decision was actually easy. I could not turn down the only chance I had to return to the NBA.

I was all set to tell Bob I'd take the assistant's job. But when he called, he asked if I would consider the head job if K.C. objected to my hiring as an assistant. Suddenly, things were really looking up.

As we got into bed that night, Cathy said, "We're going to Seattle." I told her to be careful, because I hadn't even been offered the job yet. To show how carefully she listens to me, Cathy started packing the next day. A week later they hired me.

Bob said we had to keep it hush-hush. He did not want anybody to know. But you know how well that tactic works in the NBA. Reporters were calling the next day from Seattle. I had Cathy take most of the calls. I do not know why Bob wanted to keep it so quiet, but he really did.

When we were headed to Madrid the second time, we believed we would be there for several years so we shipped over more than four thousand pounds of household goods and food. You always take food when you go to Spain. They do not have Cheerios or Oreos or cake mixes or Hamburger Helper or any of those kinds of things. So we took all that stuff with us. Now, three months later, we were moving again. So while I was trying to fly off secretly to Seattle, Cathy was planning the biggest garage sale Madrid had ever seen.

When Whitsitt called, he had no idea how badly I wanted the

job. He thought he was getting a deal because I'd agreed to work relatively cheaply, and I did not demand a long-term deal. I told him I'd take the job for as little as six months. What he did not know is that I probably would have taken the job for free. That's how badly I wanted back in the league.

There was only one hurdle to overcome. In order to accept a job in the NBA, I had to get out of my contract at Real Madrid, because the NBA recognizes foreign contracts as binding. So I had to go to the Real Madrid club president and persuade him it was in his best interest to let me go. I told him I had taken his team as far as I could and that they could do well without me, that the team was relying on me way too much. They wanted the game plan to be so cute that they never played as well as they should. He agreed, and I was a free man . . . and back in the NBA! The only detail left was that I had to say good-bye to my Real Madrid team, which was very difficult given the bond we had together.

I still have never figured out exactly how Bob Whitsitt looked at the world of basketball and, having one of the greatest jobs in the game to offer, picked me. He has said it was his recollections of the jobs I had done in Cleveland and Golden State, taking floundering teams to the playoffs. He must have remembered only the first year in each city. It certainly wasn't because of the recommendations I had received!

Once you're outside the league, you can be destroyed easily

THE RESCUE

with gossip and innuendo, especially if you do not have a good support system. You really need friends inside the league who will "talk you up"—continue to say good things about you. At that stage I did not have a lot of friends talking me up. All anyone could mention was the conclusion of my jobs in both Cleveland and Golden State. In that sense, the people who are inside the league have a big advantage over those who are outside.

I had more negative than positive comments made about me when Bob Whitsitt called around for recommendations. He was pretty honest with me about that. There weren't a lot of people recommending me when I was out of the league, even though I was winning everywhere I went.

In a lot of ways I got my first couple of jobs in the NBA when I was probably too young and too egotistical. That set the stage for a lot of bad things to be said about me—things I may well have deserved. Bob told me a lot of the things people had said about me when he was interviewing them before he hired me. Bob wanted me to make sure I knew who were—and were not— my friends. But some of my "friends" had had the chance to hire me and did not. A total stranger hired me. And he taught me to remember that. So it is not in anger that I say I do not care a lot about what people in the league think about me. I respect a lot of coaches in this league, but I will never again worry about what they say about me.

I think it's important to know who your friends are. And not

THIS GAME'S THE BEST!

many of mine are coaching in the NBA today. That's fine. I have no problem with that. I do not want to be popular. Today I just want to be a professional and be respected. That was a decision I made after Bob Whitsitt rescued me from purgatory.

On my way to Seattle, I stopped for a short time in Dallas, where I met up with my longtime friend Dan Strimple, who had been through the Cleveland and Golden State situations with me. As I got on the plane to Seattle, Dan had a few words of advice: "Do it the right way this time." I understood his point. In the past I had felt it was important to be confrontational, to show everyone I was the boss. But that approach obviously hadn't worked in the NBA. Now it was time to try and focus on coaching and push everything else aside.

On that high note, I took off. I landed in Seattle, and no one was there to pick me up. It was a hell of a way to be welcomed back to the big time! I met with Bob Whitsitt the next morning, and we ironed out the rest of the details of my contract. I was back.

When I got to Seattle, the only players I knew on the team were Ricky Pierce and Eddie Johnson. Remember, I had been out of the league going on four years. So I did not have a good feel for the team at all. Ricky and Eddie had been in the league when I last coached. Eddie has always been a great shooter, but the other guys on the team I hardly knew. I knew Benoit Benjamin,

---

but not real well. Dana Barros, Gary Payton, Shawn Kemp, Derrick McKey—I knew practically nothing about any of them.

My introduction to the team was kind of strange. I went over to the gym for a team shoot around and met the team that morning. I do not think the gym went completely silent, but there was definitely a period of awkwardness, a little strain there. They had all heard the old horror stories about how tough I was. I guess they heard how I yelled and screamed and was on the edge of being crazy.

The first couple of weeks were a nightmare. Having joined the team in mid-season, it was almost like coaching in a foreign country again. I did not know any plays, did not know what to call, did not know the talents of my players.

What it taught me was to stay simple. Make the game simple. We basically went back to some simple stuff, offensively and defensively. I told Shawn, "If you rebound and you run, I'll do everything I can to get you points." With the rest of the team I stressed defense and playing hard. I told each player he could shoot oh for ten, but if he played hard and tried to do what we wanted to do defensively, he would play. He may not play for long, but he would play!

I realized that you do not have to have a fifty-page playbook to be successful. There are certain parts of the game of basketball that you can win with, if you have the right players. The Sonics were built to run, and they hadn't been allowed to do that. Making that decision gave me my first real allies on the team, Gary and Shawn, who knew that an up-tempo game was better for them.

I learned a real lesson by coming in midway through the season. I like to tinker with the game a lot, but I still think our plan is really simple. We still focus on defense. We do a lot of switching and double-teaming, and we do run our own zone defense, even though it's illegal in the NBA. Technically, I think we're probably more sophisticated defensively than most teams.

I do not know if I guessed right or was just lucky, but after a few games, we started getting it together.

We went out and promptly lost our first game. I'll never forget it. I had been in town less than twenty-four hours when we played Portland in that first game. Portland was a good team and had been an NBA finalist the year before. It was also our archrival because the cities are so close. We played a really good game, kept it close, but could never get the shot to win it. In the end, Portland pulled it out, 93–90.

The next day's practice was the first time I could really start getting a feel for what the team had been doing. The problem with the NBA is that you can't make a lot of changes in midseason because there's no time to practice. You play too many games. The following night we played Utah and had a one-point lead with twenty seconds to go when Dana Barros got double-teamed and turned it over in the back court. Utah stole the ball and made a layup to win the game.

So I walk in with a new idea of up-tempo offense, and we start out 0–2 and we're headed for a six-game road trip to the East Coast. I was thinking about my first year in Cleveland when we were 2–19 to start the year. I did not have to wait that long to see results. The first game of our trip was in Orlando, where Eddie Johnson had a huge night and I had my first Sonics win. We would win three out of five on that road trip.

The next month, February, we were so much better that I was named Coach of the Month. But the key was that a talented team had bought into playing defense, and we had two young talents in Gary and Shawn. They were playing with a great deal of excitement. Nate McMillan was younger then and could play a lot more than he plays now, and Derrick McKey was one of the best defenders I've ever coached.

We had winning streaks of four games and five games, including big wins over the Los Angeles Lakers and the Portland Trail Blazers. The Portland game was played in front of almost forty thousand fans in the Seattle's Kingdome. It was a long way from Albany.

While some argue the NBA is a player's league, I'm a firm believer that coaching really does make a difference. No matter where you put them, good coaches will get it done, and I think there are more of them in the NBA than any other place. It's hard to win every year at a high level, but when you get a tradition going, that tradition works for you. It's very easy for me to go to practice after five years with the Sonics because everyone knows they've got to play hard or they'll never play at all. It doesn't matter if a player is a rookie or a veteran. He knows that if he goofs around, he's out. We win because we play hard, and if you do not want to buy into that, we will find someone else who will.

When I got to Seattle, the team was 20–20. We went 27–15 the rest of the year and beat Golden State in the first round of the playoffs. Better things were to come.

NINE

LOSING AND LEARNING

Unlike the many predictions made about my return to the NBA, the Seattle SuperSonics did not fall apart in 1992–93, year two of the George Karl experiment. In fact, in my first full season with the club, we ended with fifty-five regular-season wins, the second most in club history.

Then we fought through two incredible playoff series against Utah and Houston. We were actually down two games to one in the five-game series against Utah before winning Game Four in Salt Lake City and Game Five at home—after being down by ten

THIS GAME'S THE BEST!

points at halftime! That feat was actually topped by the Houston series, which ended in seven games, with the final game going into overtime!

Our Cinderella trip through the postseason continued on in Phoenix, where we met the Suns in the Western Conference Finals. That series was tough all the way, going to a fierce and final Game Seven in Phoenix. The winner of that Game Seven got the Chicago Bulls in the NBA Finals. Just a season and a half earlier the Seattle SuperSonics were a .500 team; we were now one game from playing for the world championship.

Almost everyone wanted the Suns with Charles Barkley against Michael and the Bulls in the finals. But we were right there on the edge of upsetting the best-laid plans. In that seventh game, though, the gods were not with us. We were whistled for more fouls than I thought could be called in a basketball game. In the end the Suns shot an incredible sixty-three free throws, about forty more than an average NBA team shoots in a game. The Suns beat us by only thirteen points, 123–110, and went on to lose to the Bulls.

It is easy to sit here today and say we got screwed. That's not my job. My job is to figure out how to change that problem as the game is going on. I said to my coaches two or three times during that game, "I should get thrown out of this game." But I knew that in the finals of the Western Conference, Game Seven, getting thrown out and leaving your team just wouldn't be right. In the regular season you would get yourself thrown out of that game. Your goal would have been to make sure everyone in the building and everyone watching on television knew that you were getting screwed, and it's a shame, and you were standing up for your team. You cannot do that in Game Seven, though I really thought about it before my coaches convinced me not to do it.

As miserable as it was, I stood there for every minute of that game. My only consolation was that I had a good young team that was just one win away from the finals, and we were only going to be better the next year. As much as I hate to lose, things were looking up!

To make things even more exciting, we did not stand still during the off-season. We created what I thought was the solution to our problem at shooting guard by trading for Charlotte's Kendall Gill, and adding another bona-fide star in Detlef Schrempf at the end of training camp. I could not wait for the start of the next season.

The regular season proved my optimism was well founded. We won the Pacific Division by eight games over Phoenix, the team that had ousted us the year before. We won a club-record sixty-three regular-season games. Shawn Kemp was selected as a starter for the All-Star Game, and Gary Payton as a reserve. And our defensive plan led to a league-best 1,053 steals, the second-best total in the history of the NBA.

We entered the playoffs as the number-one seed in the Western Conference, and enthusiasm was high. People weren't paying attention to the fact that Denver had played us as tough as any team in the regular season. Of the nineteen losses we had had that season, Denver had put two of them on us.

During the series I watched in amazement as we started to self-destruct. We won the first two games, and it seemed as if we were doing what was expected. But at halftime of Game Two, two of our leaders got into a shouting match that split the team. Ricky Pierce was upset at Gary Payton, and before anyone knew it, they were verbally going at it. Everyone was shaken. We were fighting among ourselves when we were up 2-0. Winning should be enjoyable and fun. But we were ruining winning.

We lost the next game in Denver by seventeen points, which did not bother me too much. But then Game Four and Game Five went to overtime, and in both games our team wasn't together when it was all on the line. We lost the series three games to two, becoming the first team in NBA history to enter the playoffs as the top seed and get beaten in the first round.

While I was shocked, it really taught me an awful lot. Everyone said an eight seed should never beat a one seed. But in the NBA, if you do not show up, you get beat by twenty. I do not care if you are playing the worst team in the NBA—if you mentally do not show up, you can get embarrassed in this league. Most coaches in the NBA have a belief that there are always three or four nights a year you've just kind of got to forget about it. You cannot take your team on for a bad effort. You just accept it wasn't your night, and if that night comes against a team you're supposed to beat, so be it. But in this instance we had three straight nights like that. We had three straight nights when we did not show up mentally. I never thought that could happen to any team I coached. It taught me we had to look for and surround ourselves with mentally tougher players.

It was the most difficult experience I had faced to that point in my coaching career. I just did not believe we could lose the series. Not even late in Game Five when we were behind. I guess I was too egotistical and thought my team was better than it was. We just forgot how to play together. We forgot how to trust one another.

I was in New York recently and Game Five was being shown on television as one of the greatest games in NBA history. I watched it for about thirty seconds, then turned it off. I did not want to see it again.

One of my theories in life is when you're in hell, what difference does it make if you're in the east part of hell or the west part of hell—you're still in hell. So rather than worry about whose fault it was that we were in hell at that moment, I needed to worry more about how to get out of there. When we lose, we all have a tendency to overanalyze. When we win, we generally do not analyze at all. I was just hoping to keep it all in perspective.

THIS GAME'S THE BEST!

I personally went into a funk. I secluded myself and beat myself up a lot mentally. It wasn't healthy. But there are a lot of things in coaching that are not healthy. I tried to figure out what I was supposed to learn, how I was supposed to avoid the same outcome if this were ever to happen again—knowing inside that it *really wouldn't* ever happen again!

Little did I know.

For the 1994–'95 season, we again added a little experience and a lot of talent. We picked up Sarunas Marciulionis and Bill Cartwright and thought we had again answered needs to take us further. And after the locker-room explosion from the Denver series, we traded Ricky Pierce, our fourth leading scorer and a great long-distance shooter.

Again, our regular-season record seemed to indicate we had done the right things. We had won fifty-seven games and finished second to Phoenix in the division. Shawn started in the All-Star Game again, and both Gary and Detlef were reserves. We won ten straight road games, more than any other Sonics team had done, and led the league in steals for the third straight year.

But this time I could sense that things just weren't right. Our home court, Key Arena in Seattle, was being renovated, so we played our home games the entire year in Tacoma.

Then, midway through the season, the friction between Kendall Gill and me became a real distraction. Kendall wanted more minutes and more plays run for him, and I let him know that, at best, he was our fourth option behind Shawn, Gary, and Detlef. He took time off during the season because he was diagnosed with clinical depression, and he sought medical treatment. There's no question that some players felt they were either with Kendall or they were with me.

Two games before the end of the year, Gary broke a finger and had a screw inserted. Nate McMillan had some medical problems. The end of the season was a tough time to have all this coming to a head.

To top it all, we drew the Los Angeles Lakers as our first-round opponent. The Lakers had beaten us four out of five times when we played them in the regular season, so they matched up well against us. They were bigger than we were. They had scorers, one-on-one guys, who could break our defense down when they had to have a basket. And they shot the three very well against us that year. To be honest, they might have been the better basketball team at that time, but no one was going to accept that possibility after we had won fifty-seven regular-season games.

We were the fourth seed going into the playoffs, the Lakers fifth. As coaches we know that the line is very, very thin, but many people think that line is huge. The numbers said we should win. The numbers were wrong.

We won Game One at home in a rout. But that was the last

game we'd win. The Lakers took three straight, and for the second year in a row we were out before most people had even started paying attention to the playoffs.

I angered a lot of people in Seattle when, a couple of weeks later, I said I would have coached the team no differently if I had had it to do over. People did not know how fragile the team was during that Lakers series. From the Gill fiasco to the negative attitudes of many players, it was not a team in sync when we entered the playoffs.

Marciulionis, Askew, and others were constantly complaining about minutes and their roles and responsibilities, so there was always a field day to be had by the press. As you might suspect, it did not take the press long to pick up on the dissension. When a player is complaining, I'm not against taking him on, and I do not think that will ever change. I like the game to be played the right way, plain and simple. I think my rules are pretty simple: Play hard, play defense, pass the ball on the offensive end of the court. You do that and in my eyes you're a talented player who will have a lot of fun playing the game for me.

It got so frustrating that I made a mistake by taking on a lot of local media guys, and they brought it back at me heavy. Given my history with the press, I should have known better. While it might feel good at the moment to say something, in the long run it doesn't help.

LOSING AND LEARNING

I regret taking on the press because I think at times it has hurt my team, it's hurt my coaching, it's hurt my communication with players. It causes a resentment and anger throughout your practices. My second year in Spain, I was wrong. I took on the press very early, and I was dead.

I do not have a lot of problems with them pointing out the negatives, because there are negatives in every game you coach. Coaches fail—we all fail. But what happens in sports is not as negative as you might think by what is reflected in the media. Still, maybe I'm not the one who should be pointing that out, because I've definitely hurt myself by taking on reporters.

A coaching friend of mine has a theory about the press: Do not let the posse form and you're okay. Because if the posse gets too big, it's going to get you. The way I dealt with the media that year, I felt the posse growing.

But that whole year I wasn't just trying to manage the press. I was managing personalities and egos much more than I was managing Xs and Os. In retrospect, I made mistakes in handling Marciulionis and Cartwright in that series. I should've played Sarunas a little more. But I had told him before the series that I probably wasn't going to play him. I had told Cartwright the same thing. My decision to hold those guys out was a result of my problems with Kendall Gill. I did not think Kendall could have stayed focused if I was taking minutes from him and giving them to bench players like Sarunas. Kendall already thought he wasn't getting enough minutes.

Well, by abandoning old veterans like Marciulionis and Cartwright to give Kendall more minutes, I probably made the right decision. But I can only say probably, because obviously it did not work.

With the cards that were dealt that year, my family was afraid that I would be fired. I knew the next morning after the loss to the Lakers that I could not act as I had acted the year before. Everybody was thinking I'd be devastated for months because it had taken me a while to get over the loss to the Nuggets. But my family could not handle another two or three weeks of me being out of control. They needed me to show stability.

The night of the final L.A. loss, Cathy called home and talked to Kelci. The first words out of Kelci's mouth were, "Is Dad going to get fired?" She proceeded to tell Cathy that she wasn't moving, even if I did get fired. She already had friends lined up to live with so she could stay for her last two years of high school.

Before I got home, a bunch of great friends called to cheer me and the family up. Coach Smith called. Larry Brown called. Del Harris, the Lakers' coach, was real good to me.

But the best was Charles Barkley, who called to boost Coby's spirits. Coby was crying when Charles got through, so Kelci had to talk to him. Charles just told both kids not to worry, that in his opinion I was a good coach and would always have work. What he did for the kids in that instance really showed Charles's class. A lot of people do not get the chance to see that side of him. I'm glad my kids did.

The kids really needed Charles's kindness because there weren't many people showing the same behavior at school. Kids are cruel. They were saying things to our kids like, "Your dad choked." They'd say things that were hard for the kids to accept.

The kids also read every word in the newspaper and watched the news. I know it was painful for them. Hell, it was painful for me. I'm big enough to handle it or not read it, or ignore it or get out of town and let it go. They could not escape it because kids at school wouldn't let them.

I've always felt you must confront losing, even when it's painful. You cannot blame losing on someone else. I've always been that way. I learned it at an early age from my grandfather. I hope through the way I handled things after the Lakers series that I passed that lesson on to my kids.

During that two-year stretch, watching how all of this affected my family, I really grew to love my role as a father. One of the hardest parts of living a coach's life is also being a part of a family. But there's no question my family has given me the base of support that has allowed me to travel the world and do what I love. I think the journey has been good for them too, because their life has been rich with experiences that have taught them great lessons.

I love being a part of my children's lives. I love going to their soccer or volleyball or basketball games. Kelci's friends call all the time asking advice about boyfriends, college choices, or school. I love to invite Kelci's and Coby's friends over after games at their schools. I've taken Charles Barkley to one of Coby's games, hoping that Barkley might inspire one player on Coby's team who I believe has great talent.

After the two first-round exits in the playoffs, some of the kids' friends were as encouraging to me as some of my coaching friends. The media, though, wasn't as kind. Among the criticisms leveled against us was that the Sonics were a great regular-season team but were incapable of winning in the playoffs. There is some truth to this. If you have more time to prepare for our game plan, you'll have a better chance to break down our defense. And when you play one team seven times over the course of twelve days, you have a lot of time to prepare.

It is also true that the playoffs are a different game. Play-off basketball is a possession game. There's not as much running, so you get fewer possessions. It becomes a half-court game. It's like the NCAA Tournament. Most NCAA games are low-possession games in which the team has one player whom they go to when things get tough. The truth is, we're not a good half-court offense. There aren't many of them in basketball,

----

and most of the good half-court offenses have a great one-on-one player named Michael Jordan or Hakeem Olajuwon or Patrick Ewing or Shaquille O'Neal. You can throw the ball to him and let him score.

I could not see us changing our game that much, because my job as coach is to design an offensive and defensive scheme around the talent I'm given. I still believe the system fits our players. It accentuates their skills and their talents, which is what a system is supposed to do for players. Now if you give me David Robinson or Patrick Ewing, you know I'll change. But we do not have a prototype All-Star center. Our best center over the years has been Sam Perkins, who is basically a power forward who can shoot three-pointers. So should I post him up every time against Patrick Ewing because that's what a conventional center does? No way.

Do I overcoach sometimes? I think I overtinker with our system, but I usually know when to stop. If I had changed our system to a slower half-court game for the playoffs just because that's what every pundit in America said it would take to win, that would have been an even greater mistake.

After the loss in the Lakers series, I think that the Sonics organization showed a strength that a lot of organizations do not show. I think management recognized that the coaching was a very strong part of the success of the team over the previous few years, despite our playoff inabilities. I was not fired, though with

----

THIS GAME'S THE BEST!

two failures like that a lot of organizations definitely would have let me go. Management did not fire me even though, in my opinion, it would have been a popular change. It was my feeling that many fans wanted me out of here.

That support made opening the 1995–96 season both easier—because I knew who was with me—and harder—because I knew all the regular-season wins in the world meant absolutely nothing to anyone. It would have been so much easier if we could have just jumped straight into the playoffs to see what we were made of.

As in the previous years, we made off-season moves intended to help us. This time I really felt we were successful.

The big difference showed up in the locker room. We had three egos—mine, Shawn's, and Gary's—that many felt needed to be paid attention to. I do not think my ego is that powerful, but other people say differently. So Kendall Gill was a problem because his ego made four. Three egos were manageable. Four were a crowd.

We traded Kendall back to Charlotte. The Hornets surprised us with their interest since they had traded Kendall to us just two years earlier because he was unhappy there. In return we got the consummate team player in Hersey Hawkins. Hawk came here and was totally into the team. He was what we needed—very unselfish. It was interesting to us that the one team that had both of them wanted Kendall back. At first it made me wonder.

LOSING AND LEARNING

But I think they were looking for a big guard. They had Muggsy Bogues and Hawk at guard. They were having post-up problems at the guard spot. With Kendall that would be less of a problem because he has a bigger, more athletic body.

A lot of people questioned the basketball sense of the move. Kendall Gill is more physically gifted than Hersey Hawkins. But Hersey Hawkins, in my opinion, is a basketball player. He doesn't take possessions off, he works the entire time he's on the floor. He doesn't pout. He understands the value of the game. Kendall plays as an athlete, and as an athlete, he sometimes has to search for the game. If he can't find his role in a game, he gets lost and causes frustration for himself, for the coach, or for his teammates.

Hawk will always mentally be in the game, and as such he will always contribute to his team. He is fundamentally sound. Because of that, his skills, though less on the talent scale, are actually greater on the big-picture basketball scale.

That trade refreshed everyone. We had two years of ego and attitude management. We had a year when there was no enjoyment, yet we won fifty-seven games. That showed me that even winning didn't bring happiness. This team was searching for fun on the court—fun that we hadn't had because of our playoff failures. Hawk came in there and kind of glued everyone together while also providing exactly what we needed, a guy who could score some points but did not need a lot of plays run for him.

THIS GAME'S THE BEST!

And he was a much better defensive player than we had ever expected.

When Hawk came in and immediately said, "Tell me what I need to do to help," I think everyone, after two years of bickering, just felt relief and joy. Hawk could put up numbers with anybody, but numbers weren't important to him.

I remember early in the year I did not use him down the stretch in one game in Portland, which we won. Immediately afterwards I went up to him and wanted to make sure he was okay. He said, "Coach, you do not ever have to talk to me after we win a game, man. It's fine." I can't tell you how good it felt to hear a professional say that, after years of having to explain myself.

Hawk and Detlef, and all the solid guys, really provided the professional leadership we had lacked in years past. As a result we stayed mentally healthy the entire season. There was never a time we were tired of playing together.

In 1996, when we got beat, we did not separate. We never pointed fingers or played the blame game. We humbled ourselves and we came together, whereas during the previous couple of years we had always separated and blamed. It was so refreshing!

Another key to our success last year was the support of fans in Seattle. They did some crazy things, like when four or five thousand people came out to the airport after the sixth-game loss to Utah in the conference finals. That really did a lot for our team.

LOSING AND LEARNING

While I was certainly feeling a lot of pressure because of the two first-round playoff losses, I wasn't alone. I think it helped that we had a whole group of guys who were in the last year of their contracts with the Sonics. All of us knew that if we had a bad year, we were all gone. Had we had only one or two guys with everything on the line, maybe we wouldn't have pulled together as we did.

That uncertainty provided room for a lot of levity among the team. If we lost a couple of games, people would joke in practice, "Well, George is gone." If a guy had a bad game, people would start making up stories about where he was going to be playing next season. If one of the guys whose contract was up had a good week, we'd all start guessing how much he was going to make the next year on the free-agent market.

The joking allowed all of us to say, "Who cares?" We knew the only thing we could do about our situation was win. Winning would take care of us. So because of that we stuck together. It was kind of cool.

It also helped that our bench became such an integral part of our game. We got enthusiasm and production from that group, a stark contrast from the prior year. David Wingate, Eric Snow, Steve Scheffler, and Sherell Ford were very important to the morale of the team.

As we entered last season, I really worked to learn lessons from our two years of first-round defeats. There are at least a couple that I felt improved my coaching.

In years past I thought I had to solve a problem immediately. When something was wrong, I set out to tinker with our game to solve it. I did not do that last year. I've learned that just keeping quiet sometimes is the wisest choice. When you've got really competitive people on your team, they often can coach themselves—certainly more than I think most coaches give them credit for. So I focused on not micromanaging our team of very good players and letting them solve their own problems.

And last year I also tried to keep my relationship with the media under control. I was professional with the press, and it was a good year. I think everyone—me, my family, the Sonics, and even the press—was fairly happy with my dealings in that area.

Everyone watched to see if I could keep that calm with the media when, just before the season, I was blistered as never before in a local newspaper story. I went into the office and you could feel everyone waiting for me to explode. It did not happen. I went home, where Kelci, who was taking a journalism class in high school, had decided she was going to stand up for me. I walked in the door and Kelci said, "Dad, you and I have got to talk." She took me out on the porch and said, "This is ridiculous, Dad. I want to do something about it." I told her not to bother. I told her that for every negative anecdote in the story, there was a positive side that just did not make interesting reading.

I had found calm. I wanted to stay focused on the season ahead. That was the best lesson of all.

TEN

SHAWN AND GARY

My experiences at Cleveland and Golden State with star players World B. Free and Joe Barry Carroll had left many with the belief I wasn't able to handle coaching a superstar. In fact, after I left Golden State, Don Nelson said I was too confrontational to coach a top-level player. He said I had to learn to keep my mouth shut and be less dogmatic in order to be successful working with a superstar.

When I walked into Seattle, I wasn't greeted with one player of that caliber. I was handed two.

THIS GAME'S THE BEST!

After five years with Shawn Kemp and Gary Payton, I think I've erased the reputation. I think they've erased a few reputations as well. And working with them, the Sonics franchise has become one of only a few organizations—Chicago and Utah are the others—to have developed two superstars from their rookie year. Most franchises buy their superstars, though I think the greatest success is had by superstars who stay where their journey started. By allowing Shawn and Gary the freedom to grow at a perfect pace for them, we were able to build a solid young foundation for our team.

Shawn is the most talented athlete I've ever been around. He's so unbelievably well put together, he can run and rebound with anybody in the world. Immediately we tried to structure our game around his skills, encouraging the whole team to run and rebound. Much about Shawn's game has developed over the last few years, but when I arrived, I knew we'd be crazy not to pick up the pace with this guy on our team.

The thing about Shawn in the early days was keeping the game fundamental. Shawn was best when he did simple fundamental stuff, two hundred times every night. When he tried to do flashy stuff, he had a harder time of it. For a guy who never played college basketball, his fundamentals were great. When his man left him on defense, Shawn instinctively went to the offensive backboard for a rebound.

If he does it every possession, his size, his strength, his quickness, and his power will give him twenty points and ten rebounds every night. Every night. As a coach, there is no greater luxury than having a guy you can count on for twenty and ten every night. Working with his career has been a great treat for me because from day one he gave us a foundation. Shawn has been the reason we have—and will continue to have—a solid base of fifty wins a year. He loves to take that responsibility every night.

It is almost as if the game comes naturally to him. There are only a few guys in the league you can say that about. Having not gone to college, where he would have had several years to mature while playing only thirty games a year, Shawn has done an extraordinary job of handling the pressures of the professional system. He's been thrown into the heat of the NBA at a pretty high level for six years now, and he's been a regular at the All-Star Game—he started in the game again in 1997. At a very young age he has been hit with experiences and pressure situations that not even older veterans can deal with. I think he's done a good job with them.

He's a good person, and he listens. Sometimes he gets distracted, but that happens to all of us. He's occasionally flamboyant. He is desirous of the big dunk. There's a machismo to it that I do not always get into as much as he does, but I see how much he enjoys it. He's not the first to love the dunk. It is simply a part of our game. There were guys in my era that did the same stuff—Julius Erving, David Thompson, and Connie Hawkins.

THIS GAME'S THE BEST!

But there are very few who make the dunk look as exciting as Shawn does.

He has also become a powerful low-post player when he's by himself. When teams do not double-team him, he dominates his opponent one-on-one. There just aren't many people who can stop him. One thing we're still working on with him is destroying that double team when it comes. The best way to do that is to create better opportunities for your teammates. If he makes the right pass every time, teams will stop coming at him with a second and even a third defender. Then, as I said, no one will be able to contain him.

Shawn's also extended his shooting range to the point where I'm not worried when he puts up the three-point shot. He won't shoot it much this year, but I think in two or three years you'll see Shawn Kemp make an awful lot of threes. The development of that longer shot usually comes with maturity. It comes when a player decides that instead of choosing to dunk over three guys, he's just going to make the easy play because his body doesn't want to take the punishment. That's why Jordan's become a jump shooter. That's why Karl Malone steps back and takes the jumper more regularly. Julius Erving became a smart offensive player at the end of his career because he could no longer do the flashy stuff. Shawn's going to get tired one day too. I just hope I'm not around to witness it!

SHAWN AND GARY

Shawn's also a mean competitor, and the exciting thing for me as a coach is he still has room for improvement on both ends of the court. Big time. He can shoot better, he can pass better, and he can learn to be a better defender—that's how good he is!

Amazingly, Shawn, at age twenty-seven, really has just two real challenges left. First he needs to win a championship, then he needs to leave his mark for Hall of Fame voters. That's extremely unusual for someone his age. If we win a championship, Shawn would have to be considered by basketball people as one of the best power forwards ever to play the game.

Shortly after I arrived in Seattle, I was told that Shawn had not respected his position on the team earlier that year. There were times when he was late for practice and even one time when he did not huddle with the team during halftime. I chalked Shawn's actions up to youth. But I wanted to make it clear I was holding him to a different standard. So when he missed a team plane that first year, I did not start him for the rest of the season. It seemed he got the message, and the veteran players appreciated the statement. He continues to have a lateness problem, but we've had a good understanding of each other ever since.

Shawn has been frustrated sometimes by a feeling that he wasn't respected or feared around the league. I have to say that the way he played against the Bulls last year in the NBA Finals, I hope he never feels that way again. Because in those six games

THIS GAME'S THE BEST!

Shawn earned the respect of everyone in the national media and everyone around the league, including the referees—which is the ultimate sign that you're a superstar.

A few years ago, after Bob Whitsitt was fired by the Sonics in mid-May, I was asked to get into the personnel side of things. My friends told me not to do it, because coaches always have a hard time in that area. It is something I'll admit is not my strength. I guess I just went overboard with it. That was the year that Shawn missed a couple of free throws against Denver in the first-round playoff loss and had a little trouble with Dikembe Mutombo. The truth is, Shawn had a great year for us, and we lost the game more because we just broke apart emotionally.

Well, the Bulls offered us the opportunity to trade Shawn for Scottie Pippen. Before I went very far in the discussions, word got out, and the deal was called off. I was embarrassed by the whole affair, to be honest. Both players are great players. Both teams would be tremendously different had it happened, and both would still be very good.

I will say now that I'm happy we did not make the trade. I will say, too, that I hope never to be making personnel decisions while coaching. I love having input—which I think all coaches do—because we are the ones who have to work with the players day to day. I want one day to run a team, but not while coaching one. I don't know how people do that. It just seems there is too much to do in both jobs to be able to do them both at a high level.

The discussions about Shawn and Pippen actually went places for a few days. But my conversations with Gary Payton about trading him never got off the ground. Gary saw to that. At the end of my first half season in Seattle, Gary and I met at the Pro Club, which is a health club in Seattle, to talk about our future.

He and I had a list of three or four things. We wanted him to spend time working on his shot. We wanted him to participate in the summer mini camps. We wanted him to get more aggressive offensively, to be more of a basketball player than a point guard. I told him I thought he played better out of control than when he was in control.

I said, "Gary, will you do these things?" He enthusiastically said he would do all those things. I said, "If you do these things, I'll never ask to trade you. I'll give you the opportunity to become everything you want to become." I'd say it has worked.

Earlier in my career I would not have been smart enough to have had that meeting. I think I would have given up. I would have said, "Get him out of here. Trade him." Thank God I was never that stupid this time around. I tell you, I'd hate to have to coach against Gary Payton, especially a Gary Payton who was motivated by the fact that we might have traded him.

Gary is like a guy who is never going to do homework in

THIS GAME'S THE BEST!

school, who is going to skip classes, yet is going to ace his exam, and he's going to write the best term papers. He's going to be the best student in your class but is always going to be distracting to you because he won't make the daily commitments that you want to keep the team positively rolling. That changed in the last year, and our level of success changed too.

Last year he was committed to playing hard every day. Last year he never took a game off. He took every game very seriously. Two years ago when you played a bad team, Gary might not be out there mentally.

Last year Gary also played through a lot of pain, which I think a lot of his teammates respected him for. People do not understand that injuries can help a team. This is one of those times. Our players knew Gary was in considerable pain. He had had a foot injury that most guys would have given two to three weeks to heal. We played two nights later, and he played. He has a back that he's managing constantly. By playing through both injuries, Gary became even more respected by the others on our team.

I'd like to rant and rave a little bit about Gary. Five years ago this guy had a lot of people who did not believe in him, from his teammates to many fans in Seattle. A number of NBA people did not think he was much of a player. Right now every team would love to have him. Right now I think he is the best point guard in the NBA. I knew in my second year—when he made a commitment to the coaching staff—that he could be an All-Star basketball player. Did I think he could be as dominating as he is today? I'm not going to sit here and say I thought that was a possibility. I thought he could become an All-Star player because of his defensive skills and his competitive nature.

What has come along with that is maturity. Every year he takes a little more responsibility in the leadership of the team. He takes a little more responsibility in the leadership of the organization. He's very articulate and an informative interview, as is Shawn Kemp. I think a big moment for Gary came last summer at the Olympics in Atlanta. I believe after the Olympic Games, Gary saw himself as a spokesperson for the league. And he enjoyed it. He's been a spokesperson for the Seattle SuperSonics in the last few years, and we think he does a great job. I think he has a little bit of Charles Barkley in him. He kind of says the right stuff and the honest stuff, not necessarily always at the right time. The power of the game is moving toward the player and the agent, and away from the owner and the coach. I think Shawn and Gary are becoming very powerful stars in our league. I hope they see that and act responsibly with their words and actions.

I think you're going to see Gary make the Olympic team again in the year 2000. I hope it's with his friend Shawn Kemp, because I think Shawn definitely deserves it, and I hope he is put into a position where he'll prove that.

What makes Gary special is his ability to take over a game offensively and defensively. Our team is often at its best when

THIS GAME'S THE BEST!

Nate McMillan moves in at point guard and Gary slides over to shooting guard. Gary is a better scorer than he is at point guard. He's a point guard, but his strength is he can score. He's not a shooter, he's not a play maker, he's a scorer, and the more he goes down the lane, the better he is passing and the better he is finishing. The less he goes in there, and instead becomes a point guard, just delivering the ball, the less our team has success.

The thing that Gary has taught me more than anything else is that competing with his level of intensity is his talent, a real talent. It's not just an attitude. He is blessed with that talent like few other athletes I've known in the last twenty years.

When Gary is kind of asleep on the court, we almost try to get another player to antagonize him, because that's what stimulates him. He gets stimulated by other people thinking they're winning the battle with him. I've seen younger players in the NBA score on Gary and yap something to him. Nothing could make me happier. I know we're okay then, because Payton will wake up and take on his challenger and usually just own him.

There have been a couple of high-profile blowups between Gary and me. The most well-publicized one came against Houston in the playoffs on national television a few years ago. We were getting blown out in the game. A couple of times in a row I tried to call a certain play. Gary didn't run the play. One time maybe Gary blew me off, but I gave him the benefit of the doubt. But two plays later I knew he was blowing me off. At times I give him that option, but only in positive situations. This was a negative situation. I called time-out and asked him what the hell he was doing. He said, "Oh, kiss off. This is bullshit."

I kind of pushed him and said, "You're just bullshit." Everybody saw it. Well in today's game, athletes do not want to be confronted in front of 15,000 people. I took him out of the game. We worked it out, and he came back. In earlier days I'd have never worked that problem out. But I keep thinking it should be like it was when I was a player. I would never have blown off Dean Smith or Doug Moe. If they called a play, I'd have run it.

Most people do not understand, though, that Gary and I are both fierce competitors, and when we walk off the court, all that is set aside.

There have been times we've had an awful lot of yelling and screaming between us, or times when the silence between us could kill. The person with the greatest perspective on my relationship with Gary is Tim Grgurich, my assistant. Grgurich believes Gary and I are tremendously alike, especially when it comes to our competitiveness. Neither one of us does well when things do not go right. When they aren't going right, I have a way—which is sometimes inappropriate—of expressing my anger and my disappointment and my frustration. So does Gary. If it weren't for the fact that we both respect each other, this could be an explosive mix. There are fewer and fewer instances each year when we go head-to-head, and we've gotten better each year at handling them privately.

The system doesn't work if there is no respect between the player and coach. If there was any question about the Atlanta Falcons last season, they were put to rest when quarterback Jeff George started cursing out his coach on national television. Now some in our society says it's okay—that's what you want in a player. That's *not* what you want in a player. You want a fighter, you want a tough guy, but you do not want a guy that disrespects authority. Your quarterback can't be out of control, undisciplined, and disrespectful.

Some might compare that episode to Gary and me. Nothing could be further from the truth. It was obvious Jeff George did not respect his coach, and the coach knew it. No matter what happens, I know Gary respects me. And no matter what happens, he knows I respect him. Completely. I am confident that if something happened to me in Seattle, Gary Payton would be one of the first players to come to my defense. The reverse is also true.

Probably my greatest Gary Payton memories would be from the end of the two seasons when we lost in the first round of the playoffs. During the series there was a tremendous amount of frustration and pressure among all of us, but when the media called on Gary after the losses, he stood up for me. He did not dump on me when it might have been the easier and more popular

SHAWN AND GARY

thing to do. Then, together, we made a special run through the playoffs last year. Gary Payton and George Karl have come together, and maybe because of that the team did the same.

Both Gary and Shawn have always felt my passion for the game equals theirs. Early on, they at times wanted to throw the ball off the backboard and throw behind the back passes and be fancier than I really felt the game should be. And to be honest with you, I compromised there. I said, "You give me the defensive attitude that I want, and I'll let you be a little goofy at the offensive end of the court."

I have said that I believed a key to our trip to the NBA Finals last year was the addition of a selfless Hersey Hawkins. But just as important to us was a decision the coaching staff made to give more of our game over to Shawn and Gary. On many nights we told them the game is going to be their responsibility to win or lose. And they reacted with great responsibility. Over the years I've had some very good players to whom we could give the game: Detlef, Ricky Pierce, Hawkins, Sam Perkins. In my years in Seattle, Sam Perkins has been as clutch a player as anybody. Detlef has been right there too. But last year every close game we gave to Shawn and Gary.

It is no coincidence that each responded with the best year of his career—and we went to the NBA Finals. Great players respond when you give them the game.

I don't want to make this sound as if these stars have peaked.

THIS GAME'S THE BEST!

They are still a combined work in progress. Gary and Shawn must continue to take more responsibility for our team, which I have every reason to believe they will. As they do, as they take each step, we will become an even better basketball team. They can't be individuals—they have to be leaders. Early in their careers their emotional outbursts separated them from their teammates, and as a coach you never want to stand behind something that separates your team. I don't see that separation as much anymore.

The Seattle SuperSonics do a lot of good stuff basketballwise. People say we're a great defensive team, and I think I have the hardest-working coaching staff in the NBA. But what made us special last year was that we *all* worked hard and we *all* played hard. And a key to that work ethic is that Gary Payton and Shawn Kemp bought into the game plan five years ago and enjoy playing hard. Every coach in the world says playing hard is the key to success. But with Gary and Shawn I've learned there are people who can play harder than other people . . . and be coachable superstars at the same time.

ELEVEN

COACHING IN THE '90S

I watched in amazement in mid-January 1997 when the Chicago Bulls were playing the Minnesota Timberwolves. The Bulls' Dennis Rodman chased a rebound out of bounds, falling to the floor. Then he kicked a television cameraman who was sitting just beyond the end line. I couldn't believe it when I saw it.

Despite the fact that good things were done throughout that game by great players, no one paid attention to those things.

THIS GAME'S THE BEST!

Every headline, every story, began with the continuing saga of Dennis Rodman's behavior problems.

The event was a perfect look at our whole league today. Good things are happening all over the league—players are donating time and money to charities, meeting with kids at Boys Clubs, or going to hospitals—yet all the attention is focused on the bad stuff. It's like having a dysfunctional child and a model child. As proud as you are of the model child—the good grades, the leadership—you almost never get the chance to praise that child because all your attention is focused on the dysfunctional child.

That's what it's like to be a coach today. We allow the negative 10 percent—it may be even less than 10 percent—of what's going on to dominate 90 percent of our time, attention, and energy.

If I could have a hardwood floor, fifty feet by ninety-four feet, and could spend my time and energy there, my job would be perfect. But I'm coaching in the '90s, leading a different type of player. That is not just my challenge. It is the challenge of every coach in America today. And we're not doing too well.

Though there has always been the problem of difficult players in basketball, we've never allowed it to get so much attention, to move out of the locker-room discussions and into television commercials.

So, unfortunate as it might be, we've all fallen into the trap of focusing on the dysfunctional. Right now there are a lot of coaches scared of what's happening to the game, worried about the prob-

---

lems in the game, who aren't happy coaching the game. They like the basketball, but they do not like what they have to deal with: the parents, the new age of recruiting, the agents, the media, the out-of-control kids. They're having trouble understanding the distractions that are closing in on the court. The court itself is still very motivating and stimulating for most coaches. The majority of us want to get back to the fun times, the laughs, the ABA-like days, the high school days, the summer-league days—the moments when competition and the love of the game come from the inside.

I've said many times that I think the college system is nearly bankrupt because skills have fallen so much—that I think the day will come when I'll see our NBA representatives in the Olympics lose a game to players from another country. It will happen in my lifetime, and everyone will be shocked.

Other countries are catching up to us not because they have better athletes or because they have great coaching. Other countries are catching us because they still focus on fundamentals. And that focus will cost us one day. I'm sure of it.

Some of these young players don't care about fundamentals. They only care about highlight reels, endorsement contracts, and rap albums. They are more interested in what their agent says than what their coach says. These players are not looking for responsibility, they're looking for excuses. Now that part of the problem is bigger than basketball. Our whole society is into ex-

---

cuses. Whether you get a speeding ticket, have an accident, or commit a foul at the end of a basketball game, everyone spends too much time on whose fault it was rather than just fixing the problem. A great athlete doesn't need to justify his failure. A great athlete has the attitude of a winner, win or lose. He doesn't have to have a justification for his failure, because in this game, somebody wins and somebody loses.

The disillusionment is so great among veteran players that they fear the end of our great game is near.

Some of today's players bring a bad attitude to the game every night. The game's strength is its discipline, its unselfishness, its cohesiveness, its ability to make five guys look as if they're playing like seven. The beauty of the game is it's a sport that has running, passing, and picking; big guys and little guys, fast guys and slow guys—and all can play well in this sport. The one thing that doesn't work in the game of basketball is individuality. You can have a team that has a good individual and it can be successful, but it can't win the championship. You can have a guy who can score forty points, and you can run every play for him, and he can beat some other teams, but I promise you you can't win a championship that way.

An example of this atmosphere is the NBA All-Star Weekend. The NBA has turned the All-Star Weekend into a show of three-point shooting and slam-dunk contests, a weekend of heavy marketing. I think the All-Star Game used to be a time of recognition and fun and old-timers getting together and celebrating the game a little bit. But now we have turned the All-Star Weekend into a marketing event that I do not think many players enjoy. The people who are excited about All-Star Weekend are the marketing and merchandising people, not the basketball people.

But the fact that All-Star Weekend is so successful shows how in touch I am with the marketing arm of the league.

Every year the power of coaches shrinks in this league because of two things: an erosion of respect for authority and a loss of respect for the team. There has been an annual decline in the commitment to the team, and there's just a lack of respect for one another. In coaching, commitment and respect are the two words you want to start with. To be a successful coach in the NBA, you need your players committed to playing hard for you. If you get that every night, most coaches will have a chance to be successful.

The two types of players that are the most difficult to coach are the excuse-oriented player and the player who thinks he's better than he is and claims he is not getting the opportunity that he deserves. I think it is already hurting the game all the way down to the high school level. A couple of years ago the father of the number-one player in Washington State told me he could not let his son play in a certain conference because the guys were trying to hurt his son and the referees had it out for him. Excuses. This is a kid who's going to go to a Division I school and his father is already rationalizing his failures. People respect people who want to take responsibility.

The thing about today's difficult NBA player is that he did not get that way just by joining the league. He did not get that way in college either. He's developing these bad habits all the way back in elementary school.

One of the kids on my son's middle-school basketball team was a very talented young guy who was irresponsible. He'd already been on three different teams in three years. He had a lazy attitude. He was inconsistent in his habits. After a practice one day I called him over. I was hard on him. I told him, "Your attitude stinks, and you are never going to be anything in basketball unless you learn how to bust your ass. If you do that, though, you could go places, because you've got talent."

A couple of days later the coach told me the kid's father had called him and basically said I did not have a right to say that. I was just shocked. My intent was to wake the kid up. Instead, he was bad-mouthing me. I figured hearing it from a professional coach might help him. I could not believe his father complained too. If I had told my father that a college or pro coach had jumped on me in a camp, my dad would have beat the shit out of me for being disrespectful. He would have taken the coach's word before mine. Then a few days later this best kid on the team quit. He was being recruited by several high schools. Now, as early as eighth grade, his parents are speculating that he's going

-- -- -- -- -- -- -- -- -- -- -- -- -- -- -- -- -- -- -- -

to get a scholarship to college. On my son's team this kid not only believed he should be the star but that he deserved a certain amount of time on the court. He was bringing that pro mentality all the way down to the eighth grade. That's just awful. The one power the coach has is playing time. If he sells that out because of favors or promises, he becomes a director and not a coach.

Coby is a sixth-grader playing on an eighth-grade team. I want him to do that because I think playing with older boys makes my son better. But what all this is teaching him is exactly what's wrong with the game today. I have gotten out of our car with Coby and my wife bitching about the coach and the referees. I have gotten out and walked home. I remember once when Coby was angry because his team lost, angry because he did not play. He started crying in the backseat, and my wife goes off on the coach and the referee. That's the wrong time to have that discussion. After losing, you should never search for excuses. You humble yourself. You accept your loss, and you think about what happened and become a better player because of the loss. When you strike out with blame within ten minutes of a loss, you're the loser. But just listen to the postgame comments after most NBA games. You'll see that these guys are doing what my twelve-year-old son was doing. Excuses are flowing in NBA locker rooms within minutes. You're not being a true competitor when you do that. You're not able to learn from the game. Losing is part of success if it is coached the right way.

-- -- -- -- -- -- -- -- -- -- -- -- -- -- -- -- -- -- -- -

THIS GAME'S THE BEST!

I love players who want to go out every day and earn their opportunity. As a coach you try to develop a comfort zone where everybody feels good about the team and what role they play. Within that zone I like to save about 25 percent of the calls I make in a game for the player who on that night has the most energy, the hot hand, or feels the rhythm. I want to keep enough freedom in the game to allow the bench player or the role player to have an opportunity to do something unexpected. I was blessed with those opportunities as a player. That flexibility—which not all coaches believe in—makes our team more difficult to coach against.

Unfortunately, it seems to get harder every year to find players who are willing to accept that role within the team. Suddenly the player is earning millions, and everybody wants a piece of him. The player has just won the lottery for the whole neighborhood. Most people say that if they were to win the lottery, the first thing they would do is quit their job. Well, a lot of players have hit that lottery, and I wonder sometimes how many of them have quit their jobs.

Today's player is suddenly surrounded by individuals who may not have his best interests in mind. I believe many current NBA players buy their friends. They buy them rather than going out and developing friendships. And the guys they buy are people who say just what they want to hear, and players are not around people who might say what they need to hear. They're making bad business deals with friends. As a coach, how do you handle it? Do you give them advice, or do you stay out of it?

I think the basketball court is becoming less important to the basketball player every year. The player's world is getting more diversified, more complicated. Those who can't manage that— who can't discipline themselves—are in for very short careers. And you can never convince them of it. I'm nervous about this trend because we as coaches are losing more and more control over what we do in our time outside of basketball. All I know is that players are now asking more often to change practice times so they can squeeze in filming of a commercial. They ask if they can miss practices altogether so they can do appearances. How can you get better on the court if you're so distracted off of it?

Too many of them do not care about what their absence does to the rest of the team. Yet it is the quality of their team that earns them status. The fans' decision to vote Gary Payton to start in the 1997 All-Star Game—just months after we went to the NBA Finals—is a perfect example. Gary had a great season the year before, but when our team didn't do well in the playoffs, he wasn't even in the top ten among guards in the Western Conference. Coincidence? I don't think so.

I haven't seen too many players from really bad teams get big endorsements. But again, you can't explain that to the players.

One thing about coaching today is you have to know what you can and can't control. We can't control money. We can control the game, the practices, the minutes a player gets. We control improvement. We control attitude. We control motivation. We control weight training. What we do will probably help players make more money if they listen. If they rebel, all they'll do is create a negative atmosphere for all of us. I still believe players in general want to listen and want to be coached. And if it is sound, solid coaching, they'll respect it. But I think the organization has to support you, and not many organizations do that anymore. That bothers me, because I believe an organization needs to support its coach until the very end, just as players should. But players are smart. If they see the coach is weakened, they sometimes create more problems. If they can divide and conquer, you're history. Obviously, this can work both ways. I experienced that when, after the first-round loss to the Lakers in 1995, Gary Payton came out immediately in support of me. He was there when others weren't.

I think a lot of coaches—not so much in the NBA as elsewhere—cheat the game too. Many coaches steal from the game. There are a number of coaches who have chosen to get along with their players, allowing them to keep their well-paying jobs. They are more concerned about their job security than they are with improving their players. I like coaching against the coaches who are searching for glamour. A Hall of Fame coach told me once that he enjoyed coaching against the geniuses and pretty boys in our sport. I'm not going to say who they are, but they know who they are. As I've said before, I do not think this game requires a lot of intellectual genius.

I acknowledge that my concerns over where all this greed is taking us are a little hypocritical. Like everyone else, I benefit from the success of this league. I'm getting richer, I'm making more money. It makes being honest and critical of the game a lot tougher.

The funny thing is that most of the superstars in the NBA today aren't '90s players. Michael Jordan, Charles Barkley, Hakeem Olajuwon, and my own Shawn Kemp and Gary Payton are examples of guys who take the game—and the responsibility—on their shoulders.

Sadly, that means that most of the '90s players I'm talking about are the also-rans of our league and the rookies. And they're the guys who will run the league when the Jordans, Barkleys, and Kemps retire. In today's game I have trouble respecting rookies because they do not come in with the attitude and professionalism that is necessary to be successful most of the time. When these kids are given between $700,000 and $2 million as a starting salary, they do not come to work every day. Sherell Ford said last year that he could be an All-Star in this league. He has no idea what it takes to be an All-Star. Young player Doug Christie once said, "I use these guys [veterans] all the time at the gym in the summertime." I told him the veterans do not play hard in the summertime. They're just there getting a run.

THIS GAME'S THE BEST!

Most rookies have to make two, sometimes three, steps of improvement in order to play long and well in the NBA. They usually have to make physical steps, get bigger and stronger. They've got to make mental steps, gaining confidence against the best players in the world. And they typically have to make some type of position change. A lot of college power forwards are small forwards or even big guards in the NBA.

Most people think the biggest challenge for a college player coming to the NBA is handling the difference in size of their opponent. The truth is, the biggest difference is in being consistent. Our players play a hundred games a year, and the great players deliver an A performance eighty games a year. In college you're an all-American if you play ten great games. If you have ten big-time games in which you score thirty points, especially in televised games, you're an all-American. In the NBA everybody on our team can score thirty points in a given game. The great ones, though, can do it the next night. In the NBA you have about two hours to celebrate, be happy. Then you're off to the next city.

As I said, I think in a lot of ways right now, the college system is bankrupt. It does not have a lot of good players. They're all coming out early to the NBA. Other than Tim Duncan of Wake Forest and Keith Van Horn of Utah this year, name me the last senior all-American who would have been one if everyone on his team had stayed. I just do not see young players helping good teams. As fine as a Duncan is, for example, he will not take a bad team and even make it a .500 club. I think good teams are going to build through free agency rather than the draft.

For years, everyone said let's build through the draft. I do not think that can happen anymore. I think it's a lot better to trade your draft picks and buy free agents that you like and you know can play. Spend an extra couple of million dollars on a guy who you know can win rather than spending crazy millions on a guy who hasn't done anything.

In 1987, I was with Golden State when we drafted Chris Washburn with the third pick in the draft. It was a flop, a bad choice. And the mistake cost Golden State just a little more than $2 million. That was less than ten years ago. That same mistake today is many more times as expensive. Why are we doing that? It's insane! There's nothing that says these guys are sure things. Now you've got an unproven risk who comes in earning more than players on your team who have given you good stuff. It just builds up all kinds of resentments.

As a result I do not think players today have as much desire to be good teammates. I have not heard a player or a coach talk about what it takes to be a good teammate in a very long time. Yet it's one of the most important things in sport. Nate McMillan, for example, is a great teammate. But there's no award for that, no competition for that at the All-Star weekend. The game will die if we don't teach players how to be a teammate.

THIS GAME'S THE BEST!

I do not think players today are as close to one another as they used to be. I think they're closer now to their agent or lawyer. Because of their great notoriety, many of the NBA's players eat 80 percent of their meals from room service in their hotel. They don't go down to the coffee shop and eat together as players used to.

Most rookies coming into the NBA believe they can change and improve their team, lead their team out of the bottom of the league. I do not know if these players now coming out of college are that talented. They're good. But they're not the old-school type of top-five players that used to be an All-Star within three years. I do not even know how many All-Stars we've had out of the top-five picks in the last five years. Other than Grant Hill, Jason Kidd, and Vin Baker, not many All-Stars have come into the league in the last few years. And of those, Hill's Detroit Pistons are the only team that's producing a good number of wins.

Recently the only players coming out of the draft that you can feel comfortable will be stars are the smaller guys, the guards. They're becoming the Allen Iversons, the Stephon Marburys. They're not the big guys who can deliver you not only wins, but wins in the playoffs. Guards can win you games in the regular season. Big guys win you games in the playoffs. The regular season has a looseness to it. It has a home-court advantage. It has an energy that goes up and down the court, where guards are more valuable. When you start the playoffs, everything becomes a half-court game and possessions become more important. In a half-court possession game, size becomes a dictating factor.

I think the young players are most interested in protecting their egos. They honestly believe the things they say: "I deserve what I get. I've earned it. Do not give me any crap about it. If you do, I'll give you an attitude." They're not willing to realize that we're all—players *and* coaches—ridiculously overpaid. That's where the rookie-coach relationship has gone to hell. Before, rookies always carried the bags of the veterans, they earned their time. They were plebes. That's gone. Today you're never going to ask a rookie to do the things we did. When I came into the league, each rookie was assigned a veteran. If the veteran wanted us to go get a pizza at eleven at night, we did it. I did those things for Coby Dietrick with the Spurs. Imagine telling some of today's rookies to go get you a pizza! A few of our veteran players have worked to develop that with younger players, and I think it's been great.

But as strong as I feel about rookies, I feel even stronger about the recent influx of high school players to the NBA. This is a lose-lose proposition. In managing you always want to get in as many win-win situations as possible. You take a young kid away from the college experience and that just hurts all levels of the game. Unfortunately, the talent of some of these kids holds great promise—look at Shawn Kemp—which has led me to have a change of attitude toward the high school players entering our league. I must admit that the kids who have come into our league in the last year—both the high school kids and the early entry players from college—have impressed me. Kobe Bryant, Jermaine O'Neal, Stephon Marbury—each has struck me as a very serious competitor who is aware of what it takes to play this game. The only guy who seems to be having a hard time with his position is Allen Iverson.

But while they've each shown great growth, the entry of so many teenagers into the draft just sounds the alarm that we need a minor-league system. We need a forum in this country where, instead of sending kids off to college to get Ds and stay eligible for a year or two and turn pro, a kid can go play minor-league basketball. We shouldn't be telling kids to fake during their college career. I want that league to be the CBA. I think the CBA can handle that. For the past ten years the CBA has provided the second-best basketball in the world, from top to bottom. The CBA All-Star team could win a gold medal in the Olympics.

Right now the rumor is that there are six high school kids considering the 1997 NBA draft. Some of them are going to fall flat on their faces. There also are some college kids who are falling flat, flunking out of school. So just because a few fall flat doesn't mean we should paint all the others with the same brush.

But there's got to be hope for those kids. If a teenager is under a pro contract for two or three years, he'll have hope. All of these kids are going to take their lumps. They're going to have failures and depressions. For them it's time for the CBA to become the minor league that almost everyone in basketball wants.

I looked the other day, and nineteen of the twenty-nine teams had fourteen or fifteen players on their roster, including injured reserves. I'll bet you another three or four will have fifteen by the time the year's out. So we're all carrying fifteen players. So why not just have a fifteen-man roster and send some players down to the minors instead of faking injuries to keep them on the NBA roster? Why not say, We're going to pay this guy because we believe he's going to be a good player, but we want him to go to Great Falls and play in the CBA for thirty games. It would be great for basketball.

It would create a totally different mentality than exists now. You'd be telling the player that he's part of your plans but you're trying to do something good for him. It works in baseball. Why shouldn't we do it? The structure for us to do this is sitting right there in the CBA.

Still, fans and owners do not understand why the great promise of these young players doesn't immediately take you to the promised land. The pressure is on from the start. As a result, that potential will take so long to fully develop that the coach, who is handed the player as a rookie, will be fired by the time the player matures. Coaches know that, and it strains the coach-player relationship from the beginning.

While those early entry players who have joined the league in the last couple of years have been impressive, I worry about some of the other players I hear are thinking about making the jump. I look at some of these guys and wonder how they think they can play pro ball. They're not physically ready. Shawn Kemp was a different situation when he came to the NBA. He's much more intelligent than people give him credit for. Shawn has always listened and always been coachable. And he's always had a strong body.

Another of my concerns is that the whole marketing of the sport today is in direct contrast to what has made the sport so marketable. It used to be the Lakers play the Celtics this Sunday. Now the promo is Nick Van Exel faces Dino Radja. It's actually shifted from the team to the name of a star: Watch Shawn Kemp face Shaquille O'Neal tonight. I read where Cliff Robinson of the Portland Trail Blazers got upset because he wasn't on the front page of a media guide. Someone had promised him that he would be on the front cover.

Consider last year's NBA Finals. In that series you had Detlef Schrempf, Michael Jordan, Gary Payton, Shawn Kemp, Scottie Pippen, and Dennis Rodman. Six guys that never get outworked. Ever. Each of those guys brings an intensity with him every night. Yet their work ethic wasn't what was being sold. What was being sold was Rodman's hair colors and Michael's and Shawn's dunks.

I liked the final-four teams last year. You had Chicago, Seattle, Utah, and Orlando. And the three teams who were most successful—Chicago, Seattle, and Utah—were the hard-nosed, defensive-minded, team-oriented basketball teams. Orlando was very talented but not very defensively oriented and certainly not very tough. I thought the Final Four was a great lesson for the NBA—a statement on what it takes to succeed. But the NBA never took it up, never talked about it. The NBA is marketing the individual, but the three best teams in basketball last year were Chicago, Seattle, and Utah, and they were the three best *teams*. Teams. They played together. And they defended their tails off.

Marketing has even become a locker-room topic among players. My players talk about Shawn Kemp's commercial and Gary Payton's commercial, rating the two. They'll even talk trash about the commercials before games. Nothing about a player's jump shot, or his drop step, or his explosion, or his shooting percentage, or his turnover-to-assist ratio. Commercials! It's all about whether your commercial is better than my commercial. "Yours was awful," Gary will scream. It just seems as if the conversations are on business more than basketball.

Take a look at the movie *Eddie,* in which Whoopi Goldberg becomes head coach of the New York Knicks. The film was made as a comedy, but it seemed too close to real life in the NBA to be comfortable. In the movie Whoopi walks into the locker room, and in one corner you've got a player talking to his agent on the phone, then you've got a guy in another corner going over his financial statement with an accountant. Beepers, headsets, everything you can imagine. It was intended as a spoof. To me, it wasn't. And I think it's going to get worse.

Look at a few of the game's heaviest hitters today:

Shaquille O'Neal: The word I associate with Shaquille is *dangerous.* He's dangerous both to his opponent and to his own team. He has not found the spirit to win a championship yet, but his size and skills put him in the top two or three players in basketball. It is unbelievably impossible to guard him one-on-one. But he's got to learn this game is a team game. He's got to learn it is a game of heart as much as it is a game of physical skill. I'd bet he'll win a championship in the next seven years. I believe that because there are years you can win the title in this league without the mental toughness you need in other years. The year that Detroit beat L.A., for example, was one of those years because of the injuries the Lakers had.

Charles Barkley: I love his honesty. I love his ability to say what should be said. He has said that's what he loves about me. I guess we're somewhat kindred spirits. But at times Charles acts irresponsibly to his team because he takes on his team and his teammates. That's unproductive. He is a proud professional when he plays the game. But he's not much of a practice player.

Dennis Rodman: He's reducing the NBA to studio wrestling. In the last two to three years he has taken advantage of the NBA's explosion to market himself like a wrestler. He's not a dumb guy, but he is making a mockery of the game. He's a fantastic basketball player, a great winner, and a challenging personality. The thing I like about Dennis is that he enjoys the responsibility of playing harder than his opponent—and he does play harder than his opponent 99 percent of the time.

Karl Malone: He is a quiet star who has accepted who he is and where he is with a humility you must admire. Because he plays in a small market like Utah, his team is unable financially to go after a championship like other teams. Yet other than one comment a couple of years ago, he's never complained. You have to feel for him and John Stockton. They have handled that situation with an integrity very few people possess.

Patrick Ewing: He is the heart of the Knicks, though Pat Riley took the glory. He is an incredible foundation. It's a shame he hasn't had the other parts around him. He has the face of an assassin. You have to like that. He has a scowl that is among the most intimidating in the league. He's a proud player. You can see there on the court that he hurts when he loses. I like that.

David Falk: Definitely one of the three most powerful men in the NBA. He scares everyone in management. I think David is a talented person who does great things for his clients. I'm not sure what he's doing is good for the long-term health of the league though. I have always had a question about David and his work with the players' union: Why do a bunch of multimillionaires need a union anyway? It's the first union of millionaires I've ever been around. I'm not sure the players need the union, but that's

THIS GAME'S THE BEST!

never been suggested. I do not think the owners are in it to hurt the players. The owners are in it to survive and make money. I just worry that all of this is going to go away someday.

Scottie Pippen: A top-five player. Has been, will be, even without Jordan. People forget that that team without Michael Jordan should've beaten the New York Knicks in 1994. I like him because he's not just a scorer. He does it all—rebounding, passing, and defending. He doesn't have a great offensive game, but he can be offensively explosive.

Allen Iverson: I love his talent, but he has a freedom to shoot the ball thirty times a game, and that's a freedom no one else in the league really has. That's great for him, but I do not know how that strategy wins a lot of games. He will improve quickly because of his opportunities, but that system will not win a championship.

Grant Hill: He's the only guy who's come along in the last couple of years that reminds me of the mental toughness and the passion and love of the game that we used to have in my playing days. I do not know him, but I love what the Pistons are doing. They play serious basketball, and they're winning above their heads because their leader is their best player, which is a quality of a championship team. That bodes well for Detroit.

Alonzo Mourning: I think he's an animal on the court. But he's an example of a player who was rewarded with a lot of money despite no history of leading teams to playoffs. There are a lot of players like that out there because personnel decisions aren't based upon winning anymore.

Kevin Garnett: I'm happy he's having success, happy that he seems as if he's got his head screwed on right. He's going to be successful. Garnett has basketball instincts that you can't teach. But I do not think he understands how early in his journey good things have come to him. It'll be a long, long time before the judgment on him will be complete. I'm positively impressed by him. I do not know him very well. I like what I've read about him and what I've heard about him, but he's got to be careful about whom he hangs out with, because he's going to be told he's successful when he probably is not and he's going to be told things are okay when they are not.

Derrick Coleman: Disappointing. Two or three years ago he was one of the greatest talents in our game. Will he get back to that? Probably not. I think once you lose your talents, lose your precision, that you do not ever get them back. You might get back to playing well, but you're never going to get back to where you once were. He set a horrible example for his teammates when he handed his coach a blank check to cover fines he would incur. You can't allow the line of authority to disintegrate.

Pat Riley: The thing about Pat Riley's teams, especially in New York, is that they are so physical that I think he has them on the fine line of cheating the rules. Riley challenged referees to make every call. He intimidated them. My problem with and my respect for Riley stem from his ruthlessness. I think sometimes Pat Riley portrays himself as a genius. As I've said before, there are no geniuses in this game. This is a game of hard work, of team-work, of discipline, of commitment. It is more a daily attitude. But to listen to Pat Riley, he represents himself as if he's smarter than we, the other coaches, are. I resent that.

I think the front offices of the teams in the NBA need more basketball people in positions of power. It seems as if the game ten years ago brought in the business guys, and the business guys got more involved with personnel. Then they got more involved with coaching. Now we've got business guys everywhere, and we do not have enough basketball guys who have gone through the trenches. We've got too many shirts and ties and not enough T-shirts hanging around the gym. I like guys in T-shirts more than I like guys in shirts and ties. Why can't we just have all basketball guys making basketball decisions? Why do we have to have these business guys messing with us? I understand it is a business, but it needs to be a game too.

For my taste, we're all getting too businesslike and definitely too pretty. The players wear their five-thousand-dollar suits. They have tailors come to the team hotel on the road. Earlier this year when we were in New York there was a lady there trying to sell furs. Can you believe that!? It's just a different game. When we used to practice in the ABA, there were times we'd get to the gym and could not get the maintenance people to turn the lights on. We were just worried about whether the doors were going to be locked and if the toilet worked and there was some water to shower. Now we worry about what investment company's going to be at the hotel and what stockbroker's going to come here, what movie production company or what fur company. It's different.

It was appropriate, I guess, that during the summer of 1996 all those business minds would go crazy rewarding players with salaries that are unthinkable. The summer was the season of business. And three months into the 1996–'97 season, I do not think mentally the league was yet back to basketball. People were still thinking money.

The business end of our game has become so important that I think some newspapers have added a business writer to their sports section. It used to be just box scores. Then you had to add a jurisprudence section. And now business. There are some writers who know more about the salary cap than I do. I liked it when it was just box scores.

History tells us there have been as many mistakes made in NBA personnel decisions as there have been successes. When you start paying the kind of money that was handed out during the summer, the mistakes can be fatal.

All that seems to be creating some distance between the players and our fans. I'm seeing fewer and fewer fans in arenas than I've ever seen before. We are an NBA Finals team, and when we go

THIS GAME'S THE BEST!

into Toronto, there are empty seats. We go into Boston, there are empty seats. Go play the Washington Bullets, there are empty seats. There are fans out there that do not want to pay these player salaries, and they know when they pay sixty bucks for a ticket, that's what they're doing—they're paying salaries.

I think that because of free agency, we've lost the ability in pro sports to build the dynasties that fans love and sports needs. I look around and I wonder whether the Chicago Bulls are the last dynasty in the NBA, a team with the ability to run off four or five championships in a row. If that is true, that is a sad statement for us to make to fans.

The fan today is getting a bad name because of sports radio talk shows. I've made the analogy that free agency is to loyalty as sports talk shows are to the true fan. Free agency has ruined loyalty, and in many ways radio talk shows and cable television have ruined the loyalty of the fan. I miss that. I miss the guy who complains and moans and groans in the barbershop or at the local coffee shop but will fight for his team.

I miss my die-hard Pittsburgh Pirates mentality. I died the day Barry Bonds didn't throw out Atlanta Braves' baserunner Sid Bream, at home plate in the National League Championship Series in 1992. It was the worst feeling in my life, because I knew that team was done. Still, next year the only team I'll study will be the Pittsburgh Pirates.

Because of radio and television, the fan today is more knowledgeable, more sophisticated, but not as loyal, not as sincerely bought into the team. You can live in Seattle and, through cable TV, be a fan of the Indiana Pacers or the Milwaukee Bucks or the North Carolina Tar Heels. Plus, so many people are moving all the time, so that erodes loyalty.

I find that little of what's said on sports talk radio is really what's being said on the street. I don't know why that's the case. I've had my ups and downs in Seattle, but the fan on the street has been wonderfully supportive of me. You wouldn't get that if you listened only to the radio. I know that free speech is a freedom of our country and should be highly respected, but the fan is important to sports. And the fan needs to feel good about sports for us to survive. If you listen to the radio, you just don't feel good about anything.

Last summer's spending spree was very disappointing because I think we're still paying a lot of unproven players too much money. I hope the system has a chance to straighten itself out before we destroy ourselves. The last thing basketball needs is to become the next version of major-league baseball. You have to remember, this game was disoriented in 1980. There were a number of NBA teams on the verge of bankruptcy back then. But we've gone from maybe the bottom of professional sports to being the most lucrative sport out there. We just might have grown too fast.

Kids today are more talented than ever. But they do not realize that this is new. They expect the attention because of statistics. Winning is not a high criterion. Why don't we list a player's winning percentage in games played? Who is the greatest winner in NBA history? I would bet it is Bill Russell. Why don't we have that stat? Why don't we have a stat for free throws made in the last two minutes of a game? Why don't we show the world who the clutch players are and who they aren't? We list the winning percentages of coaches. Winning is the reason why coaches coach basketball. Winning is why the champions are champions. Winning is why the game is so salable, why it's so competitive.

I think the reason people love basketball is that they see great athletes competing in a team structure where they have to mentally react to a lot of pressures and play with heart to win. One night their job might be rebounding. One night it might be shooting. One night it might be cheerleading off the bench. Your role changes. The great players always adapt to the game they're playing. We just need more great players.

The arrogance of the NBA really bothers me. We're all too arrogant, including myself. Everybody in the NBA thinks they're more important than they are. We're forgetting what made us successful. We were successful because we worked, we were competitive, and we had discipline, and we had an unselfishness, a commitment, and a respect for coaches that don't exist today as they did in the past.

COACHING IN THE '90S

The responsibility for all this still sits at the doorstep of the coaches. It's our fault that we've let skill levels drop, that we've let players hold us hostage. The truth is, we control the one thing they need: playing time. If we—and I'm speaking for all of us down to middle school coaches—started using the power we do have, we could change the game. The problem is that no one wants to do it, because kids today will complain to their parents and they'll all move on and find another coach. So the coach loses twice because his message was lost and now his team is less talented. And the kids keep winning.

I personally think there are more good guys in basketball than bad guys. But the bad guys have more power, more influence, and are gaining more attention than ever before. That's because of money, because of marketing. I never thought I'd see the day when commercials would be based around a player's number of technicals and ejections, like Dennis Rodman had last season. I never thought I would see the day when Dennis Rodman would become maybe the most popular player in our game because of his insane image. When we played the Bulls in Las Vegas this last year, Dennis got a louder ovation than Michael Jordan did. And we as coaches can do very little to reign him in. We are told to win games. We are not told to develop citizenship.

But we coaches can't give up—which is the easiest thing to do sometimes. We have to keep believing that players want to

THIS GAME'S THE BEST!

get better. We have to believe they want to be coached. We have to hope.

That cycle has to break for us to give this game what it deserves.

TWELVE

A FIX FOR THE GAME

During the NBA Finals last year, everyone was focused on the Chicago Bulls and whether their team, which went 72–10 in the regular season, was the best in NBA history. Those are great barroom and media questions. The problem with trying to come up with an answer is you have to start with the condition of our league before you can decide if any current team could be considered the best ever.

I have said with great confidence that our team should win at least fifty games every year. That's because there are just far too

THIS GAME'S THE BEST!

many teams out there with such mediocre talent that we should beat them consistently.

Let's face it: The NBA today has way too many mediocre teams. Mediocrity, in my mind, is what many people are calling parity. I don't agree. There are too many nights when I flip through the schedule and can't see but one game where two good teams are playing, one game I'd pay to watch. I think the NBA's very interesting when the New York Knicks play the Seattle Super-Sonics. I think the NBA is fantastic when Chicago's playing the Lakers. I think it's an unbelievable league when you've got Detroit going against Miami. I think when you've got marquee tough teams playing tough teams, I will say, "Oh, man, I've got to watch that game!"

I just do not say that very often anymore.

There are places we can look to for answers, and European basketball might be a start. In Europe the bottom teams in a league move down to a lower league the next year until they get better. So let's try it: The NBA needs to take the bottom five or six teams at the end of a season and have them play the next year in the CBA. Shrink the league, because right now we're trying to make role players into good players, good players into All-Star players, and All-Stars superstars. Because we're so short on talent, we're trying to push all the players up a level, often to levels they're incapable of achieving.

If you told an owner that his team was going to have to move down a level next year, he wouldn't put up with it. If you told owners and coaches that their bad team led by troublemaking selfish players was going to have to suffer by playing in the CBA, they wouldn't keep those overpaid troublemakers on their roster. If players start losing jobs because they're selfish and their team is not successful, younger players will learn the lesson. The only way we'll ever rid the league of the selfish players is to threaten teams that keep on rewarding those players with jobs in the best basketball league in the world.

I know this sounds incredibly drastic. I think it's time to get drastic. I'm that worried about the kids I see coming into the NBA.

I also know this goes completely against everything the NBA is planning for the future. Everyone talks about expanding the NBA into other countries. But what's the goal behind that? It is not to develop and increase the talent pool of the league.

Money is the driving force in the game today. And money is a very powerful opponent. So let's threaten the moneymakers if the game doesn't improve.

How can anyone who cares about the future of the NBA suggest expanding the league today? Everyone says that when you expand the league that more players will step up and earn a spot in it. Not true. What it means is a bunch of CBA guys will start drawing multimillion-dollar NBA salaries.

One of the problems with the NBA is a rookie can come in

THIS GAME'S THE BEST!

and get twenty-seven points and fifteen rebounds and block the last shot and make the last basket and win a game. In today's NBA he can live off of that game for twenty games. However, what you truly win on is a consistent foundation of good basketball, and when you've got players that give it one day and take it away the next, it creates a chaotic confidence.

The teams that win have a genuine confidence and know they can win almost every night. They know they've got a base of six, seven, or eight players whom they're always going to get the right stuff from. And it doesn't change. The great player, like a Kemp or a Payton, gives it every night. Now Chris Childs might play with Gary Payton one night, but Gary Payton is going to have a better season than Chris Childs. Shawn Kemp can be outplayed by Michael Smith on a given night, but he cannot be outplayed over a season.

There are a lot of times that Detlef Schrempf can get thirty-five on Tuesday night and on Wednesday he's fourth on our list of priorities of matchups. People always ask why we would do that to a guy who got thirty-five the night before. It is all about who they're being guarded by. The next night we may have Scotty Brooks covering Gary Payton. As good as Detlef is, we have to go to Gary in that situation because, one-on-one, Gary can score all the points he wants in the matchup. At the same time, if Detlef doesn't have a good matchup, I'm not going to go to Detlef. I do not care if he got fifty last night. The game tells me

A FIX FOR THE GAME

I've got to go to Gary Payton. Detlef is cool with that. Now other players would not be cool with that. Young players do not understand that. But the real pros do.

Another idea I think would increase interest in the league would be to cut the season to sixty or so games and take the month of February and play a single-elimination tournament, much like the NCAA Tournament in March. Put $5 million on the line for the winning team. If you lose, you vacation. If you win, you win a share of the $5 million. I'm sure Nike would love to put up the money. It would be a marketing hit. Have a Final Four in some city—maybe even a city like Kansas City that doesn't have a team, so that fans can get a high-quality game in their area.

The best basketball in the NBA is played in the seventh game of a playoff series. Those games are always fantastic because there's such urgency to them. Today in the NBA there just is not much urgency to most games. The NCAA Tournament is very exciting because there's urgency in every game. Lose and you go home. In a seven-game series that's not the case until the end. Hey, add another twist and say that the coach of the mid-season champion can't be fired. (That suggestion is admittedly selfish!)

Once the tournament is over, you pick the season back up and continue fighting toward the playoffs. I'll bet you'll often have a different winner of a single-elimination tournament—where getting hot at the right time is the key—than you'd have in the finals with a seven-game series deciding the champion, where depth and pure talent are more important.

This suggestion is part of the answer to another concern I have about the NBA now. Currently, there aren't enough rewards for teams. At the end of the year twenty-eight teams fail and one team is successful. The thing I like about the European system is that it has different types of championships—national champions, European champions, and Kings Cup champions. There are three or four circumstances throughout the year in which a team can come together and have a glorifying moment. The same is true in college, where you have preseason and Christmas tournaments.

Actually, it's harder to win sixty games over seven months than it is to win an NBA championship. Pete Newell wrote me a note saying that a couple of years ago. Holding your team together, motivating them to play four games in five nights several times over seven months, is harder than winning enough games to win a championship over six weeks. But through all this only one team gets to feel the reward. I think anything that reinforces the importance of T-E-A-M right now would be important for the sport.

This season a lot has been made of the drop-off in scoring in the NBA. Most people have attributed it to better defense; however, I think there are a couple of other reasons for it. The first is the increased number of calls referees are making for traveling and lane violations. I have no problem with that emphasis, because I think it will clean up the game. But we've allowed players to get away with these violations for so long now that when referees started calling them, it reduced the number of shots teams are getting. Obviously, when you reduce the number of shots, scoring goes down.

But the second and more troubling reason, in my opinion, for the falloff in scoring is that the wrong players are taking the wrong shots. Around the league today, I see the worst shot selection I've ever seen. And, if players decide to take the ball to the basket, they do not finish as well anymore. When they go to the rim, when they get close to the basket, they do not put the ball into the basket. They lose their concentration when they find contact, when they get hit and get around bigger bodies. Instead of getting a basket and a free throw for a foul, some of them are missing everything to avoid getting hit. And make no mistake, getting hit is part of the NBA. So part of the decline in scoring is due to the decline in skills, and part to the fact that players are thinking about themselves.

I understand free agency and why the players find it so attractive. But the shame is that it has robbed the game of its camaraderie. I love the game when the team has chemistry. But when drastic changes are made to clubs every year, you almost never know what piece—even what backup player—is the key to your chemistry. What you do know is when you've got it and when it's gone. That's why I've loved the Sonics last year and this year, because we seem to have that something special. We have that feeling I hope we will all remember and talk about. We have the closest thing to "tradition" you can have in the NBA.

People have suggested a number of rule changes to today's game that I wouldn't mind trying—especially if we could first try them in the CBA for a year. Allow the zone defense: Everyone in the NBA is using some type of zone defense already, but allowing the zone would make it legal and would require more of a team approach to both offense and defense. You could not just take bad offensive players and stand them above the free-throw line to tie up a defender. Whatever you give coaches, we are going to go to work breaking it down and destroying it. That's our job. After fifteen years of the rule against zones in the NBA, we're now all just trying to trick the referees. It's a boring game because of it.

Adopt the international rules of basketball: The international game has more of a flow to it than the NBA game. It may be because of the wider lane, but I think it is also because there are more little guys making the action happen.

Lengthen the three-point shot: I do not understand why we moved the three-point shot in. It's not a special shot anymore. It's a tactic. Whereas before the three-point shot required a particular talent, now everyone thinks they can do it. I do not know why we're trying so hard to make this a perimeter game. I love the game when there's passing and moving, neither of which is expected of players today, who want to stand outside the arc and yell "Money" every time they shoot a three. Chris Mullin of Golden State made a great comment to me recently, when he said he could not be drafted today in the NBA because he doesn't know how to stand still. That's a hell of a commentary about our league because he's right—there are two guys standing on almost every play.

One suggestion I would love to pursue would be allowing NBA or CBA coaches to run camps during the summers for top-level college kids. The NCAA doesn't allow it now, which makes no sense. If we want to improve the game, these kids need an opportunity to develop their skills with quality coaching and direction in the summers. All through high school, kids can go to camps in the summer. But when these kids get into college, we deny them the chance to get better. Why? It does not help anybody, any college, or the game to stymie their development.

We could hire CBA coaches, who could work with NBA staffs, which would be good for the coaches as well. And we could help these players understand what is expected of them if they plan to make a living at this game. For the top one hundred players it could almost be like an internship program for their future career choice. Other university programs do it, why not basketball? NBA clubs could fund the camps as a development tool. We'd be like Robin Hood, taking from the rich and giving to the poor!

THIS GAME'S THE BEST!

Maybe if we, at the professional level, started working with players at the high school and college age, it would reinforce the lessons that all coaches at all levels are trying to teach. Maybe it would make players more willing to let down their guard and see how much there is to learn. Maybe it would encourage some players to stay in college rather than try to jump before they should. Maybe together we could all make the game better.

THIRTEEN
1996-'97

Once you've killed the first-round playoff monkey, what do you do next? For the Sonics the answer was to finish the job we all felt we should have done last year—win the NBA championship.

There are very few teams that do not go through some off-season changes that create challenges in the early days of the upcoming year. For us, we traded Vincent Askew, and we did not re-sign two of our centers, Ervin Johnson and Frank Brickowski. To fill the hole in the middle, we went after a solid rebounder and good defender, adding Jim McIlvaine from the Washington Bullets. The signing drew a lot of attention because Jim had been a backup with Washington but was so in demand that it took a long-term, multimillion-dollar offer to get him to come to Seattle.

His addition has been a real positive, except that so much attention was paid to the money. To us, he's our version of the Bulls' Dennis Rodman: a guy who pays attention to the boards and defense and who doesn't demand many offensive opportunities. I personally think Jim makes us a better basketball team, and he allows us a versatility in the paint that we have never had before with shot blocking and post defense. I do not think we need scoring out of him. Not only do we not need him to score, it's sometimes better for him not to even worry about shots. I mean, I do not know if fans understand that, but that's what Dennis Rodman does for Chicago. Dennis Rodman never gets a play called for him. Some nights he has a great game scoring four points.

Now McIlvaine's not going to play as many minutes as Rodman does because we have Sam Perkins. Sam's a better basketball player than Mac, but Sam needs fewer minutes because he's getting a little older and sizewise he's not a center, so we'll have to figure out how to put Sam and Mac together as a great center tandem. The big plus about Jim was that as soon as he was in our camp, our players liked him. Our players like playing with him, they wanted to help him, they're talking to him. They see that he is fearless on the court physically, and all he wants to do is get better. A lot of times when you add a high-priced player, other players do not take to him. That did not happen here.

The only problem was that many people started comparing Jim's salary and statistics to Shawn Kemp's. The next thing I heard, Shawn had decided not to report to training camp. He said it had nothing to do with Jim's contract, which I believe. But it was obvious that Shawn wasn't comfortable with the whole thing—the current collective-bargaining agreement and salary cap. It was a difficult situation, because by NBA rules, the Sonics could not renegotiate Shawn's contract before next season. We could not even talk about it.

Shawn came back while we were still playing preseason games, and I think our team is veteran enough that his absence did not hurt the team on the floor. It did hurt Shawn, who took longer to get in playing shape. That meant I left him in blowout games long after he should have been sitting, just so I could get him some running time. When he's tired I play him an extra two or three minutes to burn his body a little bit. Get him that extra work.

We started the season 1–2, losing to Utah and Atlanta. We followed that with a win at Phoenix, a team in disarray that we were beating soundly until we let a double-digit fourth-quarter lead shrink to a five-point win. I was livid. We were letting inferior teams run back on us, and I was convinced that lack of a killer instinct would come back to haunt us.

I stormed into the locker room and ripped into everyone. How could this team—having gone through everything it has gone through—be this undisciplined? I wasn't satisfied after yelling at the players. So I went into the coaches' office at America West Arena and sat there yelling some more. That wouldn't have been so odd if I hadn't been sitting there all alone! My assistants came in and tried to calm me down, hoping no one else would hear my nearly insane act.

We have a theory in NBA coaching that you have six bullets—six times when we, as coaches, can really yell at our team—during an eighty-two–game season before the players just stop listening to you. At this stage we were only four games into the season, and I'd already done it two-and-a-half times.

We continued to practice every day, even when we were on the road and even when we started winning. The players were complaining but stuck with the plan, and we went on to win eleven straight. People around the country started talking about us as if we were back, as good as we were last year. To me, we weren't. I saw us going through long stretches when we just did not look good at all.

As a result I kept barking at the players to keep our intensity up. That led to a rather humorous exchange with Gary Payton during a pretty safe win at Boston. We had really bogged down, even though we had a big lead. Then we missed four layups in a row. I was yelling from the sideline at Payton when he told me: "If it's so easy, why don't you get your ass out here and do it yourself?" I figured maybe he was right and backed off a little.

Our first lengthy win streak was capped by a big win over the Knicks in New York, where Jim McIlvaine showed why we went after him this off-season. He put that big body of his on Patrick Ewing and really won that battle. Patrick shot miserably, and suddenly the stories that mentioned McIlvaine weren't highlighting how much money he was earning.

November is a month of paranoia and insecurity for most coaches. They do not know how good their teams are, they do not know how good the league is, they do not know who the competition is really going to be. The first five or six weeks of the season you are still judging teams by the previous year's reputation, so you just assume you should beat a bunch of teams that might have made some important changes. It is a nervous time because you do not want to get embarrassed.

By late December, we were 21–10, which projected to our winning about sixty games over the course of the season, and everyone was disappointed, because Utah, Houston, and the Lakers were winning more. It's hard for me to come down on a team on track to win sixty, even though others were playing better and we were not playing as well as we could.

I was a little confused by the criticism of our team. We had

THIS GAME'S THE BEST!

Shawn's decision to report late to training camp. After thirty games we had played the most road games of any team—eleven of our first sixteen were on the road, and in the NBA no matter who you beat on the road, it's a good win. We had Nate McMillan injured for most of the first half of the year. We played games in Europe. We had a flu epidemic that hit our team and was difficult to handle. I don't believe in or use excuses, but you have to recognize that there might be reasons why we are not yet where we need to be. We're not yet there, but we *will* be.

We all knew we were not yet playing at the level we had played last year. Yet in those first thirty games we had an eleven-game winning streak. We had a six-game winning streak. We turned the switch on and off, which bothered me a little. But we still played some good basketball. After thirty games we were only one game behind last year's pace.

There is a different type of pressure that we face this year. Whereas before last year we had to fight off the demons of playoff losses, now we have to battle with expectations. When we travel, everyone thinks we're great because we were in the finals. They feel we're having a good year. In Seattle the expectations seem to be higher, which I don't mind. I have them for this team myself. But we want to be judged over the course of the year, not week to week.

I have talked about last year's team possessing a special chemistry that gave us an edge. By the All-Star break in 1997, we still hadn't found that this year. We seemed to be protecting the top of the hill, as opposed to climbing to the top of the hill. There's an edge to that climb that we don't have this year.

At the same time we're much more prepared and professional in our fundamentals, which becomes very important in the play-offs, when you have to put everything else aside. Urgency has to come to this basketball team in order for us to become successful.

Chemistry was as important to our success last year as talent was. If we forget that in a six-month period, if we let our arrogance get in the way, that would be disastrous.

In the first half of the 1996–'97 season we lost two games each to our greatest Western Conference rivals—Houston, the Los Angeles Lakers, and Utah. Still, I don't think we fear any of those teams. Those other teams gained some confidence in those wins. But, come playoff time, if those teams are not the best team, that confidence can be detrimental to them. The Sonics are strong enough this year to overcome those early losses in the playoffs. Our players have been pretty honest about the fact that they haven't taken those six games as seriously as our opponents have. We face those teams two times each in the second half of the season. I hope we'll be more serious about it.

I attracted a lot of attention—none of it good—when I lost my cool during an argument with referees in a blowout of Minnesota early in the year. During the game there had been two or three instances where hard fouls were taken. The officials had

THIS GAME'S THE BEST!

called a flagrant foul against Minnesota, then a flagrant against us. I thought it was a payback call because it didn't look flagrant to me, and I was standing up for my player. There wasn't much time left in the game when one of the referees said, "Why don't you shut up—you're up by forty."

I lost it. I charged onto the floor because I thought the score shouldn't matter when you're talking about being fair. It got so bad that Terry Stotts, my assistant, and Shawn Kemp had to hold me back. When I got thrown out we were, as the referee said, up by forty in a game that was my four hundredth career win. So my explosion had nothing to do with that game specifically. It was a culmination of my frustration with the officiating in the league this year. The refereeing this year has been very difficult to handle. There is truth to the cliché that the best games are those where you hardly notice the referees. There aren't many of those games in the NBA this year.

There seem to be a number of referees—particularly the younger ones—who think people come to watch them ref.

My explosion had nothing to do with Bennett Salvatore, who tossed me. It was nothing personal, even though Bennett and I had been getting after it all night, chatting back and forth. It was just my anger inside that seems to blow about once every couple of years. Earlier in my career it blew about once every three or four months. So I'm getting better, though the $8,500 fine the NBA hit me with told me I still have a ways to go.

When I saw the video replay of my actions, I was disappointed in myself. The Sonics are getting a lot of attention right now, so that explosion made national highlight reels. For those who haven't watched me lately, they've got to think I have returned to the crazy days of old. I have been proud of the fact I haven't stuck my foot in my mouth for a while. I'm going to have to live with it.

Early in the season I joked that our team might be in need of some counseling, having ridden the roller coaster from the bottom after the Lakers series to near the top last year. After I said that, I got a dozen letters from counselors, psychologists, advisers, and ministers saying they were ready to help. They flooded me with offers.

After the blowup, another counselor wrote me a letter and said every job deserves hard work, but no job deserves to drive you crazy. It was a good piece of advice. He offered to spend a little time analyzing me. I figured it would take more than a little time, so I declined.

While we were not playing great in those first few weeks this season, I was encouraged because our practices were real serious and professional. There was a lot of discussion between players and coaches about what we were doing and why. Players were suggesting changes to the offense and defense to make it better. There was a real give and take, which doesn't happen as much as you might think in the NBA. The player-coach involvement in our workouts was greater than it has ever been in my years as a coach.

I have joked this year that our success and our length of time together has led to a power shift within the team. When I first came here I was a dictator. Then as we got comfortable with one another it became a democracy, where we shared thoughts, ideas, and power. Now all I'm left with is one of those figurehead leadership roles—like being the queen of England! I still have control of the game, and the players still respect my figurehead status.

I like our chances to get to the finals again because we learned so much getting there a year ago. Once we overcame our lack of confidence, we played well, which I think will help us immensely this next year. We know where we went wrong and will not make the same mistakes again. We have learned to trust one another and have a confidence that when it gets tough, we can figure things out.

I still think the Bulls are special and will be the team out of the Eastern Conference. I like what is happening in the Western Conference. I know the teams, and there are four that can win it: the Rockets, the Lakers, Utah, and us. And I think once we tune it up and get Nate back healthy, we're going to be able to play championship basketball. After the first two months I would grade us out at a B or B minus. There has been only one game in which we really got our butts kicked, and that was against Atlanta at hone right at the start of the season.

I think the team that comes out of the West is the team that does the best job of taking its talent and developing chemistry. And of the four contenders, I think we have a better chance of doing that than anyone. I think Utah is the most stable team but probably has the least talent. Houston probably has the most experienced talent and has experience winning the title. But the chemistry of that team seems fragile to me. The one thing about Houston is that it is an offensive team, and I think it takes great defense to dominate in this league. I still think you win with defense.

Then you have the Lakers, who probably possess the most talent but have had the least experience together and the least opportunity to develop chemistry since they haven't been together very long and their star player, Shaquille O'Neal, is sidelined with an injury.

Finally, you've got the Sonics. We loved what happened last year and are not going to forget it. The pieces are just not together yet. But we all know they're there.

The leadership of the basketball team has been turned over to Gary and Shawn, and they as basketball players have improved and are getting better. This year we are counting on them to take more responsibility than ever before. But while they are the leaders, Nate really does a great job of handling the bench, making the second guys better. He likes the challenge of motivating a bench. He helps the new faces fit in more quickly. When he's on the floor with those guys, he gives them confidence. He makes them better.

Nate's importance to this team became obvious during the one game we had him back and healthy. During one stretch in the second quarter in a game against Milwaukee, when he was in there he played so well he was a plus twenty in our plus-minus system (which means that when he was in the game, we outscored Milwaukee by twenty points). We ran better. We passed the ball better. We were more comfortable. Everybody saw what a big part of our team he was.

Then he got hurt again. Just that picture, though, showed us the future if we can keep him healthy. If Nate doesn't play, we are a different basketball team. If Nate does not play, we are still talented—I just do not know how good. When Nate was on the court we were equal to the Bulls in last year's finals. He is the best player in the Western Conference at making other people better because he is totally unselfish and committed to the game. Passing and defending are the keys to his game. Defensively he's great at making up for other people's mistakes. In football he would be a free safety. He also allows Gary Payton to be more aggressive offensively. Gary becomes our shooting guard, and so you'll see Gary curl, cut, and post his way to a lot of points.

Over the last year it seems Nate has been hit somewhat by the injury bug, which hurts him as much as it hurts us. I told Nate that we really wanted him for the end of the year, so I wanted him to take as much time as necessary to get healed. In his absence Eric Snow played well, so it was not as important for Nate to rush back.

The other cagey veteran who is a quiet key to our success is Detlef. Det's coming to Seattle in 1993 gave us the stabilizing factor for the Shawn and Gary era with the Sonics. Det probably won't get the credit for it. George Karl probably will get the credit for it. But the truth is that Det has a bigger part of it than I ever will. He came here when he was already an All-Star, and he accepted Gary and Shawn. Not a lot of players would have come here and accepted giving Gary and Shawn the team when he was still good enough to carry an NBA team himself.

He is very professional and his role as a pillar with the Sonics is as strong as anyone's. When he came to Seattle, he helped put us over the hump. We knew we had our example, our statue, that we could demand that other people live up to.

Det is a producer. Gary and Shawn are huge producers of points, assists, and rebounds, but Det is a producer in many other areas: professionalism, attitude, coachability, intelligence, passing, flexibility, versatility. Det's citizenship in his very stubborn way has been a strength that I really have respect for.

THIS GAME'S THE BEST!

A lot of times I call Det the perfect person. So much about Detlef's life is perfect that it gets to be damn annoying. He's professional. He's committed. His wife's beautiful. His kids are perfect. His cars are right. His house is to die for. It's ridiculous. This man needs flaws!

He gives a huge shot to this team on a daily basis, which I think very few stars do anymore. I'm told Michael Jordan does it. But not many more. More NBA stars need to provide that kind of commitment to develop successful teams.

I have to say there are days that—even with the leadership of a Nate and a Detlef—I wonder when our team will develop the championship mental and physical toughness of the Chicago Bulls. I know that we have it in us, but that attitude is something we have to work at. It is not yet a habit, as it is with the Bulls. Too often this season it has seemed our team lacked urgency. We play hard every night for a good portion of games. But we do not take our opponents out. At times we seem to play cat-and-mouse basketball. The first quarter we catch the mouse and we slap it and knock it out. We play with it a little bit, and then sometime later the mouse wakes up and it runs away. Then we have to chase it down again. We joke that we do not just win games once; sometimes we win them three or four times—in the same night! I would like to get down to winning them once. It's much easier on the heart.

It is also much easier on the players. We have a number of

players over thirty years of age—Sam Perkins, Detlef, Craig Ehlo, Nate, David Wingate, Hersey Hawkins, and Terry Cummings—and I would like to save them from having to play late in games, because the one thing I remember most about the finals last year was how dead tired everyone on the court was by Game Six. It is a long season, so anything we can do to conserve playing time for those guys, trying to keep them fresher, would be a lot easier on all of us.

Three years ago I said I thought the Sonics had a three-year window to win a championship and that if we did not win it in three years it might be time to break the team up. Having watched our team over these last two years, I realize the window is bigger than I had assumed. I believe with the changes that we've made to our roster and the young talent we have that we have two more years—this season and the next—before our run will probably slow. I think eventually there will be some changes necessary. That will be a good time for everybody to analyze their future. We will then be in a position where you'll have to look at the ages of some of our veterans and figure out how you replace that kind of leadership and talent.

By NBA standards we have had a pretty long run at the top over the last five years. In that stretch I have gone from a guy many thought did not deserve another shot in the NBA to the coach with the third-longest tenure with his current team. Two years from now I might even be higher on that ladder.

THIS GAME'S THE BEST!

I have loved the time I've had in Seattle. The opportunity to coach this kind of talent for this long isn't a gift given to very many guys. I have always believed I was made to coach. And no matter where it has been, I've enjoyed being able to do just that. But nothing I've done, no place I've been, has compared to these six years. I'm looking forward to the next six years, wherever my career takes me.

NBA coaching is a tenuous existence, at best, which makes it very difficult to look into the future. I have no idea whether I'll be walking the Sonics' sidelines beyond my current contract. But even if I am not around Seattle beyond the 1997–'98 season, I believe the Sonics will have a great nucleus for the years ahead. By adding a young and strong Jim McIlvaine to Gary and Shawn, we have a young foundation on whom you can absolutely build a house—and another future!